The Supernatural Transformation Series
Volume 1

The Knowledge of the Heart
An Introduction to the Heart Revolution

© **Phil Mason**

THE KNOWLEDGE OF THE HEART

© 2012 by Phil Mason. All rights reserved.

No part of this publication may be reproduced, stored in a retrieval system, or transmitted in any form or by any means electronic, mechanical, photocopying, recording, or otherwise without the prior permission of the publisher.

Unless otherwise identified, all Scripture citations are from the NEW KING JAMES VERSION © 1982 Thomas Nelson inc. Used by permission.

Scripture quotations identified as (KJV) are taken from the Holy Bible, King James Version Public Domain

Scripture quotations marked (NIV) are taken from the Holy Bible, New International Version®. Copyright © 1973, 1978, 1984 by Biblica, Inc.™ Used by permission of Zondervan. All rights reserved worldwide. www.zondervan.com

Scripture quotations marked (NLT) are taken from the Holy Bible, New Living Translation, copyright 1996. Used by permission of Tyndale House Publishers, Inc., Wheaton, Illinois 60189. All rights reserved.

Scripture quotations marked (NASB) are taken from the New American Standard Bible®, Copyright © 1960, 1962, 1963, 1968, 1971, 1972, 1973, 1975, 1977, 1995 by The Lockman Foundation. Used by permission. www.Lockman.org

Scripture quotations marked (AMP) are taken from the Amplified® Bible, Copyright © 1954, 1958, 1962, 1964, 1965, 1987 by The Lockman Foundation. Used by permission. www.Lockman.org

Scripture quotations identified (Moffatt) are from The New Testament: A New Translation, copyright © 1964 by James Moffatt, published by Harper & Row, Inc. Used by permission.

Scripture quotations identified (J.B. Phillips) are from The New Testament in Modern English, translated by J. B. Phillips. © J. B. Phillips, 1958, 1960, 1972. Used by permission of Macmillan Publishing Co., Inc.

Scripture quotations identified as (MSG): Peterson, Eugene H. The Message: The Bible in Contemporary Language. Colorado Springs: NavPress, 2002, Used by permission. www.biblegateway.com

All emphasis in Scripture quotations is the author's.

Cover design by Rosie Moulton. rosie@el-modesigns.com

Artwork by Mark Murray. "Immersed in Love." Mark Murray is a part of New Earth Tribe. Used by permission.

ISBN: 9781621660705

New Earth Tribe Publications © 2012
U.S.A. Edition - (Authorized by author Phil Mason)
Published by XP Publishing, a department of XP Ministries
P.O. Box 1017, Maricopa, AZ 85139
XPpublishing.com

About the Author

Phil Mason is married to Maria and has four adult children: three sons and a daughter. Together, Phil and Maria are the spiritual directors of New Earth Tribe: a spiritual community located in Byron Bay, Australia. New Earth Tribe was pioneered by Phil and Maria in 1998. Phil is also the director of the "Deep End School of the Supernatural" which is also located in Byron Bay. The school is a nine-month training program that equips and activates disciples of Christ in supernatural ministry. Phil completed a Bachelor of Theology at Flinders University in South Australia in 1991.

As the directors of New Earth Tribe, Phil and Maria planted the church on the foundation of the kingdom ministry of Jesus. They have sought to remain faithful to a divine mandate: not to allow their church to drift away from the call to build lives collectively upon the foundation of genuine intimacy with God and with one another in community. New Earth Tribe endeavours to be a community where everyone is committed to becoming a people of the heart. The principles and insights outlined in this book have been hammered out in the life of community. None of it is theory; it has all been comprehensively road-tested. Were it not for the twelve years of experience in building a community of people who welcome the supernatural ministry of Jesus to the heart, Phil would not have authority to address the issues contained in this series of books.

Phil is also the director of Christocentric Light, a ministry that takes teams into New Age festivals throughout Australia releasing demonstrations of the supernatural ministry of Christ. They are now seeing thousands of miracles in the New Age marketplace. Phil is also the director of the Byron Bay Healing Room and Byron Burn 24/7. To find out more about Phil and Maria and their ministry please visit the following websites.

www.newearthtribe.com
www.deependschool.com
www.philmason.org

Acknowledgements

To my wonderful wife Maria. You are such a great inspiration to me and you definitely play a crucial role in keeping me on my heart journey. I have learnt so much from you in the thirty years we have journeyed together. Thanks for your patience in the countless hours I have spent writing this series of books in the midst of what is already a hectic schedule of pastoring, lecturing, and travelling. You have supported and encouraged me all the way to continue this journey of writing to leave a legacy of our ministry together. Thank you so much for your enduring love and prophetic wisdom. I love you!

To my four adult children: Simon, Peter, Phoebe, and Toby. You guys are so amazing and I love you all so much. Without you in my life I never would have known what it means to be a father. Thanks for all the kind words you have spoken over me.

To my spiritual community: New Earth Tribe of Byron Bay. Wow! How did I end up being so blessed to be a part of such a crazy, creative bunch of wild worshippers who love the supernatural ministry of Christ? I love each and every one of you who make up this glorious community and thank you a million times over for your constant love, support, and encouragement.

To Stephen and Mara Klemich: Thank you so much for all of the support and encouragement you have given in the writing of this series of books. We are so grateful to the Father for bringing you both into our lives and we are looking forward to the years of journeying together in the kingdom of God. Thanks both of you for your generous endorsements. You're all heart!

To Ken and Linda Helser: You have both been a secret source of inspiration to Maria and me in our journey. You have such a rich spiritual legacy in your family and you exemplify a family who have fought to pursue the journey of the heart. Thanks Ken for all of your encouragement to write these books and thanks for a delightful foreword. Stay on that eighteen inch journey!

Thanks also to Randy Clark, the father of the Toronto outpouring which has given rise to the Revival Alliance movement. Thanks for the very generous foreword to my book. Thanks to Wesley and Stacey Campbell. You are such kind-hearted friends. Thanks Stacey for the endorsement and those late night conversations! Thanks to Charles and Anne Stock: we love you guys so much and are grateful to you for all of your encouragement. Thanks also to Peter McHugh, Bruce Lindley, and Fini De Gersigny for your very kind endorsements. Thanks to my editorial team who have proofread my writings and for making great suggestions in how to improve these books. And finally, the biggest thanks and praise to Jesus. I hope this book glorifies You big time and advances Your kingdom by envisioning Your followers to get on board with the heart revolution. You deserve seven billion heartfelt worshippers!

The Supernatural Transformation Series

Volume I

The Knowledge of the Heart
An Introduction to the Heart Revolution

Volume II

The New Creation Miracle
The Foundation of the Heart Revolution

Volume III

The Heart Journey
The Believer's Guide to the Heart Revolution

Volume IV

The Glory of God and Supernatural Transformation
Spiritual Dynamics of the Heart Revolution

Contents

Endorsements	7
Forewords	11
Introduction	17

Part One
The Unveiling of the Heart

Chapter 1: The Quest for the Knowledge of the Heart	27
Chapter 2: What Does the Bible Mean by the "Heart"?	45
Chapter 3: The Lack of Heart Knowledge in the Church	59
Chapter 4: Wisdom and the Knowledge of the Heart	71
Chapter 5: Kardiognostes: Only God Knows the Heart	83
Chapter 6: The Knowledge of the Heart of God	101
Chapter 7: The Intimacy Paradigm	111
Chapter 8: The Wise and Foolish Virgins	129

Part Two
Supernatural Heart Transformation

Chapter 9: Secular Psychology and the Knowledge of the Heart	157
Chapter 10: The Biblical Versus Psycho-therapeutic Paradigm	175
Chapter 11: Becoming the Head and Not the Tail	201
Chapter 12: The Implications of the "Heaven to Earth" Paradigm	215
Endnotes	224

Endorsements

Phil Mason is brilliant! In this series of books on Supernatural Transformation, he gets to the heart of the matter. Relationships (with God and people) are all about the heart. If our hearts are wounded and jaded, every area of our lives are affected. But when we get to the deeper places of God's heart, we find freedom and healing for our own hearts. This series of books provides an exceptionally clear clarion call to experience change that is real and lasting, not superficial and transitory. I highly recommend them.

Stacey Campbell
Revival Now Ministries
Kelowna BC, Canada

Phil Mason lives and thinks outside the box! He does it with profound integrity in the context of family and creative community. The book you hold in your hand is many things. It's an antidote to superficial pop spirituality. It's a beacon on the journey to the heart of reality. It's more a compass than a map, orienting you toward the depths of your own humanity and the heart of the One who made all that is. If you are drawn to the mystery of authentic living, read on! Plunge into the joy of the heart of God!

Charles Stock
Senior Pastor and River Guide
Life Center, Harrisburg, Pennsylvania

Phil Mason is an Australian revivalist and an apostolic father. He has pioneered a supernatural healing community in Byron Bay and taken the gospel of power from coast to coast as his teams impact the New Age fairs with signs, wonders, and miracles. This series of books will draw you into a deeper revelation of the finished work of the cross and your own supernatural role in the end time harvest.

Fini de Gersigny
Founder, Jubilee International Church
Sydney, Australia

Phil Mason is one of the greatest Christian thinkers in this generation. His unique teaching ability of combining great theology with practical Christian living results in this great resource – *The Supernatural Transformation Series*. I highly recommend that you buy these great books. They will be a point of reference for decades to come.

Bruce Lindley
Regional Director of Harvest International Ministries
Gold Coast, Australia

Phil Mason has captured a compelling call for God's people to have experiential knowledge of God's love and ways that re-orientate their inner world. *The Knowledge of the Heart* is an extraordinary journey carved out of sound biblical interpretation and life changing ministry. You will discover the absolute importance of allowing Jesus to fulfil His assignment to heal your heart.

Peter McHugh
Senior Minister, Stairway Church Whitehorse
Melbourne, Australia

"Speaking from the heart," "heartfelt," the "heart of the matter," "being bottled up," and many other familiar sayings are not just sayings any more. The realization that we need to develop people's hearts and character is upon us. We are seeing the church return to Jesus' ministry to the heart for the development and transformation of people from the inside out. In our corporate consulting work, organizations have now adopted our "Smart with Heart" leadership and development programs globally. Phil's books are a read and re-read series that will stretch, strengthen, and lengthen your heart for bigger things.

Stephen Klemich
Founder of "HeartStyles" and "Achievement Concepts"
Sydney, Australia

Phil's series of books are a practical and biblically based exploration of Christ's ministry to the heart. Pursuing an understanding of the issues of the heart will bring you to a deeper intimacy with God. In seeking to recover the biblical knowledge and teaching on the heart, this series of books will lead you on a journey to reconciliation with the heart of God.

Mara Klemich, Ph.D.
Co-founder of "HeartStyles" and Consulting Psychologist
Sydney, Australia

Foreword
By Randy Clark

Phil Mason's new four volume series, *The Supernatural Transformation Series*, boldly endeavors to deepen the work of revival and renewal in the church. This series will take us back to the foundational issue of the supernatural miracle of regeneration and deepen our understanding of the experience of justification and sanctification as they relate to this miracle of regeneration. God has given us a brand new heart and this a supernatural act of heaven invading earth.

Volume I: ***The Knowledge of the Heart***, is a strong biblical exploration of the importance the Bible places upon the heart. Phil gives us a thorough understanding of the meaning of "heart" in the Bible, and he calls the people of God to fully embrace the heart journey that Jesus intends each of His followers to recover. Jesus lives within what Phil identifies as the "intimacy paradigm." We are called to embrace this paradigm from the heart and allow it to revolutionize and transform our lives from the inside out. Intimacy is a journey of the heart.

Volume II: ***The New Creation Miracle***, focuses upon the issue of conversion and the reality that God has performed the miracle of giving us a brand new heart. Phil notes, "The new creation is the cornerstone and foundation of all Paul's theology. If Paul could communicate just one thing to believers it would be the revelation of the new creation." Phil emphasizes that this new creation event is an actual new "creation" of God; it is not just a theological fact but also an experiential reality. It is a supernatural reality, not just an abstract theological reality. In fact, the new creation miracle is the focal point of heaven invading earth.

Phil engages deeply with the subject of the finished work of Christ in this book. He asserts that the distinction between the finished work in our spirit and the unfinished work in our soul is part of the subtext of the New Testament. Phil focuses on how this revelation explains the paradox that calls us sanctified, yet we must pursue sanctification; we are cleansed but we must pursue cleansing. Phil's insights into the relationship between justification and sanctification are important in maintaining a clear biblical balance. The author also places a strong emphasis upon learning how to align ourselves with the fact of our co-crucifixion with Christ. Phil emphasizes that God cannot do this for us; we must develop the art of coming into alignment with the finished work of regeneration through the weapon of our will.

Volume III: *The Heart Journey* focuses on the New Testament concept of "entanglement." Phil identifies seven major arenas of entanglement revealed in the New Testament: the entanglement of Satan's lies, the entanglement of sin and selfishness, the entanglement of the tree of knowledge of good and evil (meaning entanglement in the law – the mind-set of external rules and regulations), the entanglement of worldly temptation, the entanglement of wounded and broken emotions, the entanglement of demonic infiltration, and the entanglement of physical biochemistry. This last sphere of entanglement explores the implications of living in a physical body that has been deeply corrupted by the fall.

Volume IV: *The Glory of God and Supernatural Transformation*, focuses upon the theme of deep-level heart transformation explored through the lens of the ongoing supernatural kingdom ministry of Jesus to the hearts of His people. This book places particular emphasis upon Jesus' ministry of healing the brokenhearted, a theme that has been greatly neglected by the church. In seeking to deepen our understanding of this ministry, Phil gives us five keys to healing the brokenhearted. These are biblical revelation, the call to forgiveness and repentance, experiencing the glory of the Father's love, and discipleship. He follows up his emphasis upon healing the broken hearted with a similar emphasis upon the issue of demonization and the Christian, and the biblical ministry of demolishing demonic strongholds. Phil explores the biblical relationship between broken-heartedness, demonization, and the new creation.

Phil concludes the last book in his series by presenting a bold vision for the kind of supernatural freedom that Jesus intends to bring into the hearts of His people. He explores God's intention to bring many sons and daughters to glory and to fill our hearts with the glory of the Lord. This transformation from glory to glory can only be experienced as Christians receive the fullness of the kingdom ministry of Jesus. Phil emphasizes that this deep level of heart transformation is entirely supernatural and predicated upon the church entering into the fullness of the charismatic paradigm so that we can receive all that God is seeking to pour out upon his Church. The glory of the Lord can only cover the earth as Christians are fully awakened to the supernatural ministry of Jesus, and as they step into the fullness of the new creation miracle.

It is Phil's desire that this series of books will lay a strong theological foundation for training God's people in the nature of New Testament heart ministry; a supernatural ministry that calls the church to focus on deeply transforming the hearts of God's people. This is not just through an abstract "positional righteousness," but through the experiential gift of righteousness. Not just through the experience of justification, but through the ongoing experience of the joy and freedom of sanctification. Phil also recaptures the emphasis of the early church that emphasized that the ministry of the Spirit—being filled with the Spirit—is intended to be part of the regeneration experience.

I believe Phil Mason's new four volume series, *The Supernatural Transformation Series*, is an important contribution to the present day theological discussion that is seeking to refocus our theology upon the Bible. This series allows the Bible to speak for itself, not allowing it to be interpreted through historical theological paradigms, whether they are Protestant, Roman Catholic, Orthodox, or even Pentecostal traditions. This is a read that will enlighten all of us. But more than that, it will challenge you to embrace the heart journey as you seek to live from the heart in pursuing a deeper intimacy in your relationship with God and with one another. It is time for a widespread heart revolution in the church!

Randy Clark
Global Awakening
Mechanicsburg, Pennsylvania
www.globalawakening.com

Foreword
By Ken Helser

It so happens that I was working on a book called *Living from the Heart* at the same time Phil was studying and putting together his early manuscripts on a book on the heart. Once while I was staying in his home, he gave me a copy and I nearly did not sleep the entire night because I was so engrossed in his material.

I am thrilled that Phil is finally getting these messages published. Why? Because when I first announced I was working on a book about the heart, more pastors than I could count confronted me with the question, "What exactly do you mean by the heart?" They had no clue and were so confused, which got me digging. Digging deep I asked, "Lord, what do You mean by the heart?"

Wow! That's about the same time I read Phil's material. He put it into words so simple that I got pumped and now I'm more pumped than ever. I could finally put in words what the "heart" meant not just to me but to God. Yeah! Thank you Phil, for digging out what God really means by the word "heart." May this series of books go all over the world, for the "heart of the matter" is what matters most to God.

At our ministry, A Place for the Heart, we've run a school for years now called *The Eighteen Inch Journey*. It has transformed the lives of young folks from all over the world, yet we are constantly asked, "What do you mean by calling it an eighteen inch journey?" We always answer, "Oh, that's the distance between your head and your heart." Still, without careful digging and revelation you cannot know what that means.

So, finally my good friend Phil Mason has poured not just his head, but also his whole heart into this series of books on the heart. I've read them and highly endorse him and his work, for every believer must make the *Eighteen Inch Journey* in order to live from the Spirit and not the head... and if you are not American, that's called the *45.7 Centimeter Journey*.

A wise man once said, "You cannot give what you haven't got any more than you can come back from where you haven't been." The reason I can read Phil Mason's messages on the heart and come alive from his revelation is not necessarily because he's brilliant, but because he's lived everything he's written. Nothing that Phil gives is second hand information, but the overflow of living from the heart of God! Read Phil's work and you too will understand that you are reading a man's heart that has encountered the very heart of God first hand.

Ken Helser Ministries
A Place for the Heart
Sophia, North Carolina, USA
www.aplacefortheheart.org

Introduction

"In the beginning God…" With the first four words of the Bible we are launched into the ultimate adventure of discovery. What a profound revelation. We are not alone in the world! We live in a universe charged with glorious supernatural realities! God takes His own existence for granted because He has lived with Himself for all eternity past. But He certainly doesn't take our existence for granted. Human beings are His glorious workmanship, and His eyes are upon us continually. We are the focal point of His loving gaze, not galaxies, stars, or super massive black holes!

For the believer, our attention is directed toward the glory of God and the fascination and wonder of His divine nature and the majesty of His being. But God's attention is fixed firmly upon you and me. God has always been seeking the affections of our heart. In the words of one of my favorite worship songs, "God is a lover looking for a lover, so He formed my heart!" The existence of God and the existence of human beings made in the image and likeness of God is a "tale of two hearts." The crucial question we face as we contemplate our existence has always been, "Where do we stand in relation to the heart of God?" How does our heart respond to this glorious Being who reveals Himself as a deeply affectionate Father and a lovesick Bridegroom?

Our salvation is of supreme importance to God. Jesus came to seek and to save that which was lost. But in the midst of the unfolding drama of the fall and human redemption, God's personal quest is to bring us back to our heart and to reconnect our heart into a vibrant, living relationship with His own heart. "Deep calls unto deep"

(Psalm 42:7). But this side of heaven, our salvation doesn't necessarily guarantee this outcome. The gift of salvation ensures our heavenly destiny and frees us from the horror of an eternal existence separated from God. It's incredible to know that our eternal destiny has been forever settled because of our faith in Christ. But unfortunately, many Christians seem to have missed the heart of the gospel message.

From heaven's perspective there is nothing more tragic than a Christian who has accepted Christ as Saviour but has not yet learned how to engage with the heart of God and to reconnect with their own heart. Something has gone terribly wrong! Christians who are still disengaged from their own heart become trapped in a twilight zone of intellectual belief without experiencing the true essence of their redemption: the glorious riches of a deep heart connection with God as their loving heavenly Father and with their newfound family in Christ. Christians who are stuck in an expression of faith that is oriented exclusively around intellectual beliefs have missed the point entirely.

The essence of salvation is a heart that has been profoundly awakened to the extraordinary love of God, catapulting the believer into a journey of deep heart transformation and the discovery of what it means to be doubly alive. Not only to be alive physically, but also to be alive spiritually. We who have been supernaturally born from above have been made "alive to God," yet it remains for us to lay hold of the fullness of this glorious new life in Christ. The fullness of true spiritual life is expressed in a heart that has been gloriously awakened and that feels again. A "Christian" with an unfeeling heart is a contradiction in terms.

This series of books has been written with one primary objective: to reconnect Christians with the heart of God and thereby with their own heart. When we encounter the lavish love of the Father it awakens our heart to a new found fervency and passion. God wants us to be a people of the heart. He doesn't look upon outward appearance, but

Introduction

He looks upon the heart. He desires a family of sons and daughters who also look upon the heart, just as He does. This is a fundamental core value for God, and we are not complete until it becomes a core value that we are willing to fight for. Salvation is infinitely more than an issue of our eternal destiny. It is a glorious reconciliation between the hearts of men and women, who were once completely lost, with the Lover of their souls.

Reconnecting with the heart ushers us into the Divine romance between the bride of Christ and our heavenly Bridegroom. Our eternal destiny is to become lovers of the Bridegroom. John the Baptist described himself as a *"friend of the Bridegroom"* (John 3:29). The Greek word for friend is *philos*, which means *one who loves* or an *intimate lover*. Did you know that the Bridegroom calls His disciples *lovers*? John 15:15 states, "No longer do I call you servants, for a servant does not know what his master is doing; but I have called you *friends* [*philos*]." As the Bridegroom King, Jesus has the privilege of defining the relationship, and He chooses to call us intimate lovers.

This intimate love relationship that we are called to is a heart connection between friends who are deeply bonded in love. This heart connection is the essence of our union with Christ, and it radically transcends a mere intellectual understanding of the nature of our relationship. We cannot tolerate getting stuck on the journey to becoming lovers only to be trapped in our heads with nothing more to hold onto than a mere intellectual apprehension of what our relationship is intended to be. A casual student of the Bible would appreciate that love is intended to define our relationship with God. Jesus said the greatest of all commandments is to love the Bridegroom with all of your heart, soul, mind, and strength (Matthew 22:37).

The heart is the most important subject in all of Scripture. It is with the heart that we believe and are saved, and it is with the heart that we learn how to engage in an intimate relationship with God. Every human problem is essentially a problem of the heart. When I did a postgraduate Diploma of Ministry at Bible college, one of my lecturers said, "*The heart of man's problem is the problem of the heart!*" That idea riveted my attention and captivated my heart, so much so that as I have journeyed through life, all of my life's experiences end up pointing me back to the issues of the heart. God wants us to keep the main thing the main thing. He commands us to keep our heart with all diligence because out of it flows the "issues of life." All of the major issues that touch our life point us inexorably back to the issue of the heart. "Above all else, guard your heart, for it affects everything you do" (Proverbs 4:23 NLT).

I enjoy watching a good movie with my wife. Cinema is a popular medium for the modern day storyteller and the best movies that truly move me tell stories that centre on the theme of getting back to the heart. Talented authors and script-writers move their audience with heartfelt themes about rediscovering the value of love, restored relationships, and the power of family and fatherhood. These stories awaken deep themes in people's hearts that move us to tears by tapping into feelings that have often been glossed over by the pain of human existence. Getting "back to the heart" is a primal theme that stirs us all deeply. Sometimes it seems like the world of cinema can inadvertently be more prophetic than the church.

This book is the first in a series of four books that has been designed to equip everyday believers to live both from the heart with God, and with one another. Each chapter functions as a building block, following the principle of "line upon line and precept upon precept," so that the reader can develop a comprehensive understanding of the call of God. To embrace the heart journey and to navigate life from the heart. In order to live from our heart we need to be reconnected with our feelings and feel God's heart toward us. We also need to be able to know what God is doing in our heart in any season, so that we can cooperate with Him in the journey of

Introduction

supernatural transformation. He doesn't leave us in the dark because He always seeks to upgrade our intimacy!

We can only know God's heart (and our own heart) through the lens of biblical revelation. Viewing life through the lens of Scripture is to see reality through the eyes of God. God articulates in His Word a perfect description of reality so that His people can also be equipped to step into a clear and accurate perception of reality. As we are progressively immersed in an ever-expanding knowledge of the Word of God as it relates to the issues of the heart, we are equipped to know the heart of God and subsequently our own heart. We are also equipped to minister to the hearts of others and to join Jesus in His glorious kingdom ministry to the heart. Jesus is the ultimate prophet and He always speaks straight to the issues of the heart.

Every Christian is invited into the prophetic realm so that we can learn to flow in the gift of prophecy. God wants to teach all of us to prophesy. The prophetic gift, as we will see in this book, is all about the knowledge of the heart. If we are to grow in the prophetic, we must also grow in our knowledge of the heart of God and of the human heart. So this series of books has also been designed to equip believers in their growth in prophetic ministry. The Word of God is the only foundation of prophetic ministry.

No one can be called a prophet if they lack a basic knowledge of the Word of God. But once a believer is solidly grounded in the Scriptures, they are uniquely positioned to know God's true heart and voice as it pertains to the situations they face in everyday life in all of their relationships. That is because the Bible is all about the heart! The biblical knowledge of the heart is the foundation on which prophetic people can discern what God is seeking to do in their own heart and in the hearts of others. This unique sphere of revelatory knowledge is foundational to the prophetic. The most prophetic people I have ever met have been—like Jesus—people of the heart.

My wife, Maria, has taught me that there are head prophets and there are heart prophets. She is a prophetic trainer and the Lord showed her this important distinction. Head prophets are big picture prophets who perceive the sweep of God's redemptive purposes. They can have an extraordinary knowledge of the Word of God. They understand the times and the seasons and can discern where we are historically in the grand scheme of things. But heart prophets are a different breed. They have been endowed with profound wisdom and insight into the human heart. They can perceive where people are in their spiritual journey and what the Father is saying to them. They can look into a person's hearts and call out the treasure, and they know how to encourage the people of God to step into their prophetic destiny, because they can spiritually perceive people's destiny and call it out.

I have written this book for all true lovers of the Word of God. My strongest gifting is in teaching and unpacking biblical revelation. I seek to equip the church in an intimate knowledge of God so that we can know Him personally and understand His ways. I am continually astonished at how much profound revelation is packed into the Bible! I have immersed myself in the Scriptures for over thirty years and to my mind, this particular field of revelation regarding the biblical unveiling of the heart is the richest of all veins of revelation in the Bible. It encompasses the unsurpassed revelation of the heart of God and the revelation of the human heart. This includes not only the revelation of the heart of fallen humanity, but also the incredible revelation of the new heart that God has given His redeemed sons and daughters. God is all about unveiling the heart.

In part one of this book, we explore the knowledge of the heart both as a rich theme of biblical theology and as a prophetic call to deep intimacy with God. In part two we examine some of the contemporary "naturalistic" challenges that have arisen within the church and are currently hindering the development of this field of supernatural

Introduction

revelation. Part two concludes with a prophetic call to recover the fullness of the supernatural paradigm of heart transformation. My prayer is that your life will be deeply enriched and enlightened as you enter this glorious vineyard of revelation. I hope you enjoy reading these chapters as much as I enjoyed writing them. May Jesus receive the reward of His sufferings, not only by seeing an unprecedented global revival in this generation, but also in seeing a widespread heart revolution in the church, which He set in motion two thousand years ago. Only a widespread heart revolution will fulfil Jesus' prayer in John 17 that we all may be one, just as He and the Father are one.

This mystical *oneness* defines the heart connection between the Father and the Son with all those who are in Christ. As Luke said in his description of the early church, "Now the multitude of those who believed were of *one heart* and one soul" (Acts 4:32). There are still vast unexplored dimensions of intimacy waiting to be discovered by Christians who have embraced the call to become a people of the heart. Like John, all of us have the potential to lay our head upon Jesus' breast and listen to the beating of His heart.

We know that "In the *beginning* God" but in the *end* it's both you and God in mystical union, celebrating the restoration of hearts that can once again delight in the intimate love of our heavenly Bridegroom King. The capacity to enjoy an intimate heart relationship with God is a glorious creation in itself. Relationship is a powerful gift. Becoming a person of the heart brings us back to the very essence of our existence. It is the ultimate core value! Let's become part of the heart revolution that Jesus brought to earth two thousand years ago.

Phil Mason
Byron Bay,
New South Wales, Australia
April, 2012

Part One

The Unveiling of the Heart

In part one we will explore the biblical revelation of the heart. The heart is one of the most significant themes of biblical revelation. God deeply desires to reveal the fullness of His heart to humanity. He also desires to restore fallen men and women back to their own heart, leading them on a journey to recover the lost knowledge of the heart. We see through the supernatural ministry of Jesus that God is deeply committed to showing us our own heart so that we will recognise our desperate situation and cry out for salvation. But once we have received Christ, He continues to minister to our heart, gently drawing us into the intimacy paradigm. We have been predestined for intimacy. The deepest places in the heart of God cry out to the deepest places in our heart as God draws us into intimate fellowship. What is utterly amazing is that God has made Himself so accessible to His sons and daughters. We can know the heart of God for us and we can live a life that is attuned to the very heart of our heavenly Father. As sons and daughters who have been born from above, we have been invited into the ultimate spiritual journey: the journey of the heart.

Chapter One

The Quest for the Knowledge of the Heart

Gavin and Paula were in deep trouble and all of their closest friends knew it. Gavin had been an elder in his church for eighteen years and he was widely regarded as a capable teacher. But the tension in his marriage was palpable. At first it seemed that they were just facing some ordinary marital challenges, but the atmosphere of mistrust and resentment was now leaking like a poison. Their attendance at the regular dinner parties they had enjoyed with friends for years had become increasingly awkward and embarrassing.

Gavin had a nasty habit of putting Paula down publicly every time she expressed her opinion on theological issues. But Paula had a feisty streak and she was not going to allow Gavin to humiliate and walk all over her. Many times she would also publicly expose Gavin's weaknesses and inconsistencies to her friends. Sometimes it felt as though they were trying to get everyone at the table to take sides. If this is what they were like in public then what must their marriage be like behind closed doors? They were never open about their struggles so all of their friends were left asking the same question.

Gavin and Paula were now in the epic battle of their lives. They had believed in Jesus since they were teenagers but neither of them could be described as people who addressed the hidden issues of their heart. Gavin came from a Christian family that never discussed anything deeper than sports and politics. Paula came from a secular family where all of the women were extremely controlling and judgmental. There seemed to be a lingering bitterness in everyone in her family of origin and as the years rolled by, Paula also became increasingly prickly in all of her relationships. Gavin and Paula's story is typical of millions of believers who inwardly refuse to do the hard work of a heart journey. As far as they were concerned, believing in Jesus and committing their ways to the Lord ought to have taken care of all of the inner struggles they knew lay just beneath the surface.

Writing on the subject of the heart has been unusually challenging. So many subjects can easily be intellectually mastered, but not this one. I have been deeply stirred by the Spirit of God to explore this subject for the past seventeen years and this series of books is the product of that journey. Writing on the heart has been a tremendous growth experience that has stretched and challenged me to the very core of my being. But many times I have not felt qualified to write on this subject, even though I could see a desperate need for more literature in this field.

If living from the heart and being a person who is on a genuine heart journey with God and others is the standard that qualifies someone to write on this challenging subject, I have frequently wondered if my own personal failures in walking out this heart journey have actually disqualified me to speak on this subject. As I think about the great challenge of becoming a truly heart focused person, I am infinitely more conscious of my failures than I am of my successes.

All of us who have sought to follow Jesus have, at one time or another, pondered the degree of success or failure with which we have navigated the heart journey. It is hard to escape the fact that Jesus is all about the heart. I think all of us, if we are truly honest with ourselves, would be far more conscious of our failures to love, to truly forgive, to show mercy, to live free of judgment toward others, and to walk in true intimacy with God and others than we would be of the measure of our success.

But if we approach this subject together as a company of "glorious failures" in the profound challenge of navigating the heart journey, then we can grow together as we learn from our own failures and the failure of others, and as we move ever closer toward the goal of becoming a company of people who truly live from the heart. One thing is certain: God is committed to each of us becoming people who are deeply concerned with the issues of the heart, because He is.

If failure is part of the package on this glorious journey (and believe me, it certainly is), then we must be willing to explore our failures so we can move out of a place of perpetual failure and into a place of success. It has often been said that we learn more from our personal failures than we do from our successes. If this is true then we must be prepared to look squarely at those areas in our heart where we continually fail. Our goal is to overcome and break through into a place of navigating life from the heart. We are called to live a life of love, just as Christ loved us, and this must become our lifelong pursuit. We must embrace the fight in this arena until we overcome.

The truth is, every Christian I know, including myself, has lived a life of failure in the heart journey. Not only do we come to Christ as complete failures, but we are faced with the challenge of pursuing breakthrough in our hearts. This pursuit leads us on a journey where every inch of territory is fiercely contested by the powers of darkness. Inch by inch we are claiming territory in the Spirit where we have been faced with giants and mountains, just like the children of Israel in the conquest of Canaan. In fact, the narrative of the conquest of the Promised Land serves as a powerful metaphor of the heart journey of the Christian. The taste of victory is sweet and it is meant to inspire us onward in a journey of conquering the "me" mountain. There are giants in the land but we have exceedingly great and precious promises that stir us to be overcomers: people who refuse to walk off the battlefield.

I was profoundly impacted a number of years ago by the words of a prophetic friend, Graham Cooke, who said, "We are all Pharisees in the process of being healed." His point was that all believers have pharisaical attitudes in their hearts toward others. We are all on a journey of being healed of judgmental attitudes. We can move forward in becoming a people who learn what it means to be merciful, just as our Father in heaven is merciful. That statement by Graham Cooke highlights a principle that is equally true in many other areas of the Christian life. We could just as truthfully say that we are all failures in the heart journey on our way toward success. This is the direction in which we are all hopefully heading, and this series of books will be a tool in the cultivation of that personal heart journey.

My own heart journey has been deeply challenging. I come from a family where emotional expression is almost completely absent. Dissociation from feelings has been a hallmark of my parents, their parents, and their parents' parents. As a first generation believer, I have had a mountain of heart issues to overcome and I am still walking through a deep, healing journey to become a whole, emotionally expressive husband, father, and pastor.

The greatest challenge for me personally has been in cultivating a heart that truly feels so that I can stop moving through life in exile from my true interior feelings. My core relationships have been littered by a thousand omissions. This pattern of chronic omission is rooted in the dissociative patterns that have characterized my family of origin for untold generations. This has been one of my greatest giants and I am still learning how to wield the slingshot to bring it down.

The Bible describes the *unfeeling heart*. David said, "They have closed their unfeeling heart" (Psalm 17:10 NASB). Paul called this condition "being *past feeling*" (Ephesians 4:19). Both David and Paul were describing a widespread syndrome in their generations. This has been the experience of my generational predecessors. It has been a long-term challenge for me to break out of this all too familiar pattern of being "stuck" emotionally and constantly failing to express my heart. The only real comfort on this journey is in knowing that the vast majority of men in my nation, including men in the church, are struggling with the same thing.

These are the kinds of things we all must overcome if we really desire to be a people who live from the heart – a people who are learning how to move out of the arena of endless omissions and into the realm of expressed love. All of us have giants to slay and mountains to conquer, but if we lay down our weapons and try to walk off the field of battle, we end up digging a deeper hole in which our personal strongholds only become more deeply entrenched. Unfortunately, these kinds of deep heart issues don't just automatically go away.

Every heart issue that we foolishly sweep under the rug comes back to haunt us in the form of relational problems that inevitably percolate to the surface. Because God tenaciously pursues the enemies of love inside our hearts, He has a "ways and means committee" to bring these things into the light. Our task is to come into alignment with our assignment to keep our heart with all diligence and to continually pursue true heart freedom.

Jesus and Heart Ministry

The theological paradigm that forms the context for this series of books focuses upon the ministry of Jesus to the human heart. The more we can lay hold of a vision of what it is that Jesus is seeking to achieve in each of our hearts, the more we can step forward in our own heart journey and open up our hearts to the ministry of Jesus. I think Jesus is looking for one thing and He summed it up in one word: **love**. Jesus' teachings on love and healthy relationships are the profoundest and deepest revelations of the true nature of love ever to be articulated in the entire history of humanity. No one has even come close to defining what real love looks like apart from Jesus, and love is the ultimate issue of the heart.

I have been in ministry for almost thirty years and during that time I have spent a considerable amount of time reflecting and meditating upon the nature of Christian ministry. The purpose of this series of books is fairly straightforward. My central thesis is that the Holy Spirit is incredibly intentional about revealing the glorious ministry of Jesus Christ to every believer, and that this supernatural ministry is directed exclusively toward the human heart.

The ministry of Jesus is entirely supernatural from beginning to end. As this supernatural ministry is revealed to us by revelation, it is intended to become the paradigm for all true New Testament ministry. Receiving the revelation of Jesus' supernatural ministry to the heart is absolutely indispensable for every Christian. Only this can personally position us to receive the fullness of His ministry into our own hearts and teach us how to participate with Him to effectively minister into people's lives.

Every single disciple of Christ has been called to receive the fullness of Jesus' kingdom ministry and to be trained in kingdom ministry. The pathway to successful kingdom ministry that transforms people's lives is to first receive Jesus' ministry into our own hearts. Then we become qualified and equipped to minister to others. Jesus said, "Freely receive, freely give." It is in the receiving that we are equipped to give.

For those of us who are passionate about ministering to others, the ministry of Jesus defines the very nature of what we call "ministry." This glorious ministry of Christ is, in its essence, a ministry that is directed to the depths of the human heart with the goal of transforming every human heart into full conformity to the heart of Christ. As the archetypal prophetic minister, Jesus came into the world to reveal the true heart of God to humanity and to also unveil the broken and sinful hearts of fallen men and women. Without at least an entry-level revelation of the fallen condition of the heart we cannot be saved. God reveals the presence of sin so that we choose repentance. But even once we are saved, Jesus continues to minister to our hearts as He unveils the free gift of the new nature within us. He systematically strips away every trace of our old sinful nature through the power of the cross.

Jesus' ultimate purpose was to initiate a profound reconciliation between the heart of God and the hearts of those who have been alienated from His heart through the fall. The ultimate goal of this reconciliation is to fully reveal the heart of Christ in all those whom He has redeemed. "For whom He foreknew, He also predestined to be conformed to the image of His Son, that He might be the firstborn among many brethren" (Romans 8:29). Whatever we may think of when we think of the concept of prophetic ministry, at its core the nature of the prophetic is to *reveal the heart.* As Simeon prophesied to Mary concerning Jesus, "This child is destined to cause the fall and rise of many in Israel, and to be a sign that will be spoken against, so *that the thoughts of many hearts will be revealed*" (Luke 2:34-35 NIV).

Much has been written in recent years on the recovery of true prophetic ministry. When it comes to the nature of the prophetic, I think it needs to be clearly established that Jesus is the supreme pattern of all prophetic ministry. His ministry defines for all Christians in every age the very nature of true prophetic ministry. The truth is that there is really only one ministry, and that is the ministry of our great God and Saviour, Jesus Christ. His ministry is specifically focused upon the human heart: your heart and mine. Above all things, I want my ministry to so closely resemble the ministry of Jesus that people will feel as though Jesus Himself has ministered to them through me. But my feeble desire to manifest His ministry is comprehensively eclipsed by the unbridled passion of Jesus to manifest His glorious, heavenly ministry through His church.

The Holy Spirit relentlessly seeks to bring a deeper unveiling of the ministry of Jesus to a church that has experimented widely with all kinds of self-styled ministries. This experimentation with humanly conceived models of Christian ministry is in itself an admission that the church has been, to a certain measure, blinded to the unveiling of the glorious ministry of Jesus. Jesus' supernatural model of ministry is from above, but there are many expressions of ministry within the church that are purely naturalistic and earthly. His ministry is so incredibly awesome that it causes all earthly concepts and expressions of Christian ministry to appear utterly bankrupt.

What we desperately need in this hour is a Holy Spirit inspired revelation of the heavenly ministry of Jesus Christ and the courage to lay down all ideas and concepts of ministry that do not conform to His glorious ministry. Jesus is seeking to manifest His magnificent kingdom ministry through His church, which is His body on the earth. Jesus is completely focused upon heaven invading earth and there is no greater target for His mission than your heart and mine. What does it look like for heaven to invade our hearts and for the supernatural power and love of God to flood our interior life?

The Fullness of Kingdom Ministry

Jesus not only seeks to express this supernatural ministry through His church, He wants to manifest the ***fullness*** of His ministry through the church. He is not satisfied when we only receive or participate in a fraction of His ministry, because a fraction of His ministry will only accomplish a fraction of His purposes. Throughout church history the followers of Christ have, for various reasons, experienced significant difficulties embracing certain aspects of the ministry of Jesus. Whether people have had problems with the ministry of casting out demons, prophetic ministry, physical healing, or the healing of broken hearts, the results have been the same: significant aspects of the person and work of Christ have been neglected. The end result is that Jesus has not been revealed in His fullness through the church.

The Apostle John said, "From the *fullness of His grace* we have all received one blessing after another" (John 1:16 NIV). God's intention is to manifest the fullness of the grace-based ministry of the Lord Jesus Christ to His church in order that the church may grow up into the measure of the stature of the fullness of Christ. It takes the fullness of Christ revealed to us to release the fullness of Christ in us and through us. "For in Christ all the fullness of the Deity lives in bodily form, and you have been given fullness in Christ" (Colossians 2:9-10 NIV).

I am thoroughly gripped by this concept of the fullness of Christ. Paul refused to let go of the vision of the New Testament people of God coming "to the unity of the faith and of the knowledge of the Son of God, to a perfect man, to the measure of the stature of the fullness of Christ" (Ephesians 4:13). He worked tirelessly toward the fulfilment of this vision. But for the church to corporately lay hold of the fullness of Christ it necessitates a massive transformation in the hearts of God's people.

It is the nature of the prophetic to unveil the fullness of Christ. I am convinced, after years of reflection on this matter, that the fullness of Christ is manifested through the fullness of His supernatural kingdom ministry to His bride. But to the extent that we have historically lost the full apprehension of His ministry, to that same extent we have forfeited our right to grow up into the measure of the stature of the fullness of Christ. Nowhere has this tragic loss of the fullness of Christ been more evident than in the church's historical rejection of the prophetic ministry of Christ as He seeks to heal and transform the depths of the redeemed human heart.

"Evangelicalism" is the term we use to describe that stream of Christianity that believes in the divine inspiration and authority of the Word of God. But ironically, evangelicalism has historically stumbled when it comes to embracing certain aspects of the supernatural. Because the evangelical stream of the church has had significant problems embracing supernatural ministry, their theological or philosophical prejudice against the supernatural has inadvertently obfuscated the *very nature* of the fullness of Jesus' ministry. Jesus' ministry is 100% supernatural!

The Holy Spirit deeply desires to restore the revelation of the supernatural ministry of Christ to the church so that the church can receive the fullness of His transformational ministry. Jesus came to radically transform the human heart, not only from the power of sin but also from what Jesus called a *broken heart*. This is a significant part of His ministry. Jesus said, "The Spirit of the Lord is upon Me, because He has anointed Me to preach the gospel to the poor, He has sent Me to *heal the broken hearted*, to proclaim liberty to the captives and recovery of sight to the blind, and to set at liberty those who are oppressed" (Luke 4:18).

Jesus came with a specific assignment from the Father to heal our hearts. There is an awakening taking place amongst true believers that Jesus came to heal the brokenhearted. This awakening is slowly leading to deep-level healing in those broken places in our hearts that have hindered us from growing in the true depths of intimacy with the Father that the Scriptures promise us. According to Jesus, the fallen human heart is not only bound by sin, it is also deeply wounded and broken. When we come to Christ, God's intention is that all of us embark upon a journey of deep spiritual freedom, not only from sin, but also from the effects of living in a sinful world where people have been deeply wounded by other people who have been bound by sin.

Jesus revealed that He came into the world not only to cleanse our hearts from sin but also to heal and make whole those aspects of our inner lives that have been shattered and wounded through living in the midst of a sinful world. The evangelical church has excelled in calling humanity to repentance from sin and in declaring the power of the blood of Jesus to cleanse our hearts from all sin. But they have been significantly neglectful of the ministry of healing the brokenhearted. It is reminiscent of what the Lord said to the apostate shepherds of Israel, "The weak you have not strengthened, nor have you healed those who were sick, *nor bound up the broken*, nor brought back what was driven away, nor sought what was lost" (Ezekiel 34:4).

Almost without exception, most evangelicals since the Reformation have proposed a one-dimensional solution to a two-dimensional problem of the human heart. More often than not, the glorious prophetic ministry of healing broken hearts, exemplified in the historical ministry of Jesus, has been completely missing from the church's ministry repertoire.

For many years I have been on a specific spiritual journey. It has been a theological and experiential journey that has been shaped and moulded by years of practical ministry experience to broken human lives. I am the pastor of a local church that cares for broken people. Along this journey, I have stumbled upon a depth of revelation into certain aspects of the ministry of Jesus that desperately needs to be recovered by the wider church. In my personal quest to fully recover the "lost ministry of Jesus to the human heart," God has gradually imparted a deeper understanding into certain dimensions of ministry that have been completely overlooked by many historical and contemporary streams within the church.

As I have engaged in on-going ministry within the church, it has became increasingly apparent to me that I have struck a rich vein of biblical revelation that has scarcely been explored in evangelical circles. I have drawn extensively from the insight of others but I have also pursued my own personal quest to plumb the depths of these themes in the Scriptures in order to develop a comprehensive biblical theology of the fullness of Jesus' supernatural ministry to the heart. In part, it has been this ever-widening scope of revelation that has inspired me to write on the subject of the transformation of the heart.

The recovery of the theology and practice of the ministry of healing the brokenhearted is a story that has to be told. I have no desire to try to write something that has already been written by someone else – that would be a waste of time. If someone else had already said it loudly and clearly, I wouldn't have spent the past seventeen years developing this teaching into a series of books. Throughout this time, I have thoroughly searched the spectrum of Christian literature in this field, and I came to realize that I had a unique contribution to make to the literature on the supernatural transformation of the heart. I believe that the material in these volumes will be greatly beneficial to all who are pursuing the recovery of the supernatural prophetic ministry of Jesus to the heart.

A Systematic Theology of the Heart

The more I have sought to explore what the Bible has to say about the human heart and the ministry of Jesus to broken hearts, the more I have realized that there has never been written a systematic theology of the heart. A theology like this would be for the benefit of all who seek to excel in ministering to the deep heart issues that all human beings face. There are systematic theologies that have been written on almost every subject in the Bible but a systematic theology of ministry to the heart has, to the best of my knowledge, never been written. As this realization dawned on me, I felt increasingly compelled to write something in this area as a contribution to the church's growing understanding, not only of the broken condition of the human heart, but also of the glorious kingdom ministry of Jesus to heal the heart.

I am personally persuaded from the Scriptures that Jesus has the answer to every problem facing every human being no matter how shattered and broken their lives have become. Jesus is the "skillful heart surgeon" who has come to operate upon our hearts in order to transform us into His very own image. His ultimate goal is to completely remove every remaining trace of the old "heart of stone" in our lives and to establish us in the free gift of a new heart, which is really His heart beating and pulsating within every one of His redeemed children. As image-bearers, we have always been called to be an expression of God's heart.

The new heart that God has come to give us is in reality, the very heart of Jesus! We are called to be partakers of the divine nature. Every born again believer has already received this new heart but tragically, very few Christians break through into a place of actually expressing it and living from it. There is an urgent need for every single believer to grow in their revelatory understanding of the miracle of the new creation and the reality of the new heart that Jesus has already given them at the new birth.

This series of books is a journey into the very heart of supernatural and prophetic ministry. We will seek to explore what the Bible has to say about the human heart as we seek to carefully craft a systematic understanding of the ministry of Christ to the heart. Each chapter represents a significant building block that will ultimately lead us toward a more comprehensive understanding of God's vision to transform our lives. God builds "line upon line, precept upon precept" (Isaiah 28:10); every truth is built upon the foundation of other truths. I have intentionally designed this book to build precept upon precept in order to broaden our understanding of this glorious biblical theme. As each building block is set in place we will ultimately arrive at a clear and comprehensive vision of the condition of the fallen human heart and the Christian journey of supernatural heart restoration and transformation.

We are living in a day when knowledge has vastly increased, just as Daniel prophesied (Daniel 12:4). Humanity is experiencing an explosion of knowledge on every frontier. But I am convinced that the knowledge of the heart is truly the last frontier of human knowledge. This is due in part to, as Peter said, people seek to remain wilfully ignorant (2 Peter 3:5) of certain confronting realities. The heart journey is clearly the road less travelled! To journey on this road requires the serious inconvenience of being repeatedly torn out of our comfort zone and stretched into new frontiers of spiritual growth in our pursuit of intimacy with God and with the community of God's people.

The knowledge of the heart grows inside each of us as we experience a deeper unveiling of the heart of God, as we grow in our understanding of the heart of fallen humanity, and as we discover the revelation of the new heart that God has put within us. But the knowledge of the heart really explodes inside of us when we embrace the personal call to walk out a true heart journey with Jesus and with His redeemed community. This is a life skill that every one of us must learn how to cultivate as we pursue intimacy with God in the Secret Place and as we learn what love looks like as we build community with one another. This is the essence of Christian discipleship.

The knowledge of the heart is ultimately an expression of the mind of Christ. Jesus has a perfect knowledge of the heart of the Father and of the human heart. He knew what was in people because He could see straight into their hearts. But this knowledge is not cultivated as a mere intellectual pursuit. It flows out of our intimate pursuit of the heart of Christ. Jesus said that our thoughts proceed out of our heart (Mark 7:21). If this principle is true, then the mind of Christ is a product of the heart of Christ. The Word proceeds from the heart of the Father. With Jesus, the heart always takes pre-eminence followed by the mind.

The point is: we cannot put the cart before the horse! If we seek to grow in our knowledge of the heart, we must be committed from the outset to a deep heart journey with God and our brothers and sisters in Christ. This authentic heart journey will ultimately produce in us the very mind of Christ, and we will gradually arrive at a profound, cumulative knowledge of the heart. The more we grow in this revelatory knowledge of the heart, the more we will participate in the mind of Christ, because Christ is unswervingly focused upon issues of the heart.

Embracing the real heart journey with God is the pathway to true spiritual intelligence that is rooted in a glorious combination of the heart and the mind. God looks upon the heart (1 Samuel 16:7)! There is something about this concept of the knowledge of the heart that brings us to the very essence of true spirituality. This is a lofty theme that is worth the attention of every true follower of Jesus. If we embrace the invitation to the road less travelled, we will end up thinking brilliantly because we have made the heart our number one priority. Christians who display the greatest emotional and spiritual intelligence are those who do not hide from their own hearts but pursue a lifestyle of conformity to the heart of Christ at whatever price.

The knowledge of the heart flows inexorably out of a strongly relational paradigm. This field of knowledge is fundamentally inaccessible to those who reject a relational paradigm with God and with His people. We are discussing a body of revelatory knowledge that only flows out of a life that pursues intimate love for God and intimate love for His people. We are called to love God and to love one another, and this radical lifestyle is predicated upon a commitment to get on the same page with God. And as we have seen, God looks upon the heart!

My goal has been to keep the teachings in this book simple and biblically based. My hope is that it will be useful to many Christians who are on a similar quest to recover the fullness of the prophetic ministry of Christ to the heart. If you are hungry to experience the fullness of the ministry of Jesus in your own life and to participate with Jesus in this glorious ministry to others, then this book is definitely for you!

Chapter Two

What Does the Bible Mean by the "Heart?"

For the Lord does not see as man sees; for man looks at
the outward appearance, but the Lord looks at the heart.
(1 Samuel 16:7)

Ben was only four years old when he turned to his dad and asked, "How can God know everything?" Ben's dad, stuck for words, hesitated, then simply replied, "Well, because He is God!" Have you ever been asked this question by an inquiring young mind that is wrestling with the biggest questions of life? The omniscience of Almighty God is an unfathomable mystery that radically transcends the capacity of our human minds to comprehend, much less to explain. But the very reality of the existence of God confronts us with the revelation of a Being who is not bound by human limitations because He is infinite.

God knows all the stars by name (Psalm 147:4). He knows how many grains of sand there are in the earth. Jesus tells us that even the very hairs of our head are all numbered (Matthew 10:30), from which we may infer that God even knows the exact number of atoms and sub-atomic particles in the entire universe. "Nothing in all creation is hidden from God's sight. Everything is uncovered and laid bare before the eyes of Him to whom we must give account" (Hebrews 4:13 NIV).

The Knowledge of the Heart - Part One

The writer to the Hebrews wrote this sentence right on the heels of the previous verse, which, interestingly, wasn't discussing sub-atomic particles. The previous verse tells us, "The word of God is living and powerful, and sharper than any two-edged sword, piercing even to the division of soul and spirit, and of joints and marrow, and is a discerner of the thoughts and intents of the heart" (Hebrews 4:12). The author of the book of Hebrews was pondering God's comprehensive knowledge of the human heart. God's attention, we are told, is *not* riveted upon the galaxies and the stars but upon the human heart, upon every human heart simultaneously. As God said to Samuel, the Lord "looks upon the heart" (1 Samuel 16:7). David was meditating upon this incomprehensible divine omniscience when he threw his arms in the air, completely overwhelmed!

> O Lord, You have searched me and known me. You know when I sit down and when I rise up; You understand my thought from afar. You scrutinize my path and my lying down, and are intimately acquainted with all my ways. Even before there is a word on my tongue, behold, O Lord, You know it all. Such knowledge is too wonderful for me; it is too high, I cannot attain to it. (Psalm 139:1-6 NASB)

The overwhelming revelation of God's absolute omniscience forms the very foundation of prophetic ministry. Whenever a follower of Christ participates in the joy of His prophetic ministry, they are participating in a tiny fragment of the omniscience of the all-knowing God. A *word of knowledge* (1 Corinthians 12:8) is a small fragment of the *spirit of knowledge* that rested upon Jesus (Isaiah 11:2). The basic building blocks of prophetic ministry are found in what the Scriptures call the *elementary principles of Christ* (Hebrews 6:1).

The elementary ingredients of Jesus' ministry consist of a comprehensive knowledge of the heart of the Father and an intuitive knowledge of the ways of the human heart. Without these fundamental building blocks in place we cannot participate in the prophetic ministry of Christ. The basic skills of a prophet consist in the revelatory knowledge of the heart of God and a revelatory knowledge of the actual condition of a person's heart.

The more we know of God's heart the more we gain prophetic insight into the present condition of someone's heart. Prophets are called to interpret both the heart of God to humanity and the hearts of the people to whom they are ministering. They are uniquely gifted as ministers of reconciliation to re-connect the hearts of men and women to the heart of God. Therefore, a basic knowledge of the heart is foundational to successful prophetic ministry. The perennial watchword of the prophets is "intimacy."

I am convinced that all New Testament believers are invited to participate in the prophetic ministry of Christ. "The testimony of Jesus is the Spirit of prophecy" (Revelation 19:10). I love the way the New Living Translation puts it, "For the essence of prophecy is to give a clear witness for Jesus." The outpouring of the Holy Spirit results in the sons and daughters of God prophesying (Acts 2:17-18). Paul encouraged all believers to pursue the gift of prophecy and said, "You can *all* prophesy" (1 Corinthians 14:31). Moses said, "Oh, that all the Lord's people were prophets and that the Lord would put His Spirit upon them!" (Numbers 11:29).

Whenever we accurately interpret the heart and mind of God to others, we are prophesying. However, not all believers who prophesy should be considered "prophets." The term prophet is reserved for those who hold the office of a prophet in a local church because they are strongly established in the gift of prophecy. These people are also widely recognized by their local church for their integrity and their personal track record in prophetic ministry. New Testament prophets will always speak according to the Word of God, and mature prophets will accurately reflect the heart and mind of God as it has been revealed in the New Testament. It is a prophetic person's greatest privilege to participate in a body of heart-focused knowledge that comes exclusively from above.

Technical Biblical Language

If our prophetic ministry is to be entirely biblical, we must think in terms of biblical ideas and concepts. We need to define our terms and get our language straightened out if we want to accurately reflect biblical language. The language of the Scriptures speaks in terms of the human *heart*, the human *spirit*, and the human *soul*. In this second chapter we will explore the nature of the human heart and its relationship to the biblical concept of the human spirit and soul. We will also discuss further the biblical idea that the heart is the focal point of God's dealings with humanity.

The knowledge of the heart, both of the heart of God and the heart of man, is the highest form of knowledge in the entire world. Paul declared that "all the treasures of wisdom and knowledge" are hidden in the person of Christ (Colossians 2:3). Jesus knows and understands the human heart, and He invites us to share in this knowledge so that we may participate with Him in His ministry to the human heart. Knowing and understanding the ways of the human heart is not an end in itself – it is a means unto an end. The end goal is to be equipped to be co-workers together with Christ, ministering to the deepest issues of people's hearts so that we can lead people into true spiritual freedom.

If the human heart is the exclusive focus of God's attention, it must be extremely important. The concept of the heart is unquestionably one of the most important themes in the entire Bible. The term *heart* or *hearts* is used approximately 975 times in both the Old and New Testaments (NKJV). This should tell us something about the significance of this theme. The Bible tells us all about the heart of God and the heart of man. Everything in Scripture ultimately hinges upon the way the human heart responds to the revelation of God's heart.

In the Old Testament, the Hebrew word for heart is *leb* or *lebab*. It is used for the physical heart of a person, which was regarded as the centre of the physical body (see 2 Kings 9:24). This is the heart that pumps blood throughout our body. But the word is also used figuratively to describe the centre or depth of something, for example, "the *heart* of the sea" (Psalm 46:2). It is also used figuratively to describe the core of a person's inner being. This is by far the most common usage of the word in the Bible. In the New Testament the Greek word for the heart is *kardia*. The term is used both literally, to describe the physical heart, and metaphorically, to describe the inner person. As in Hebrew, so also in Greek – it was an easy transition to speak of the heart as that which defined the invisible, spiritual dimension of a person.

Peter used the term "the hidden person of the heart" (1 Peter 3:4). The hidden person of the heart is the **real** person as distinct from how a person might appear outwardly to others. The use of the term heart to describe the *inner depths* or interior of a person is as old as the Scriptures. The term is now universally understood, even in secular society, to speak of the inner core of our being. Even in everyday language people talk about how they feel in their heart. Every love song in every generation sings about the feelings of our heart.

Both the Old and New Testaments use a number of synonymous terms to define the spiritual dimension of a person in contrast to the outward or physical person. The following terms are synonyms for what the Scriptures describe as the heart:

1. The Inner Man

That He would grant you, according to the riches of His glory, to be strengthened with might through His Spirit in the inner man (Ephesians 3:16).

For I joyfully concur with the law of God in the inner man (Romans 7:22 NASB).

Therefore we do not lose heart, but though our outer man is decaying, yet our inner man is being renewed day by day (2 Corinthians 4:16 NASB).

2. Our Innermost Being

Who has put wisdom in the innermost being or given understanding to the mind (Job 38:36 NASB)?

Behold, You desire truth in the innermost being, and in the hidden part You will make me know wisdom (Psalm 51:6 NASB).

He who believes in Me, as the Scripture said, "From his innermost being will flow rivers of living water" (John 7:38 NASB). ["Out of his heart…" NKJV]

3. Our Inmost Being

Praise the Lord, O my soul; all my inmost being, praise His holy name (Psalm 103:1 NIV).

My son, if your heart is wise, then my heart will rejoice; my inmost being will rejoice when your lips speak what is right (Proverbs 23:15-16 NIV).

4. Ones Inner Being

Therefore my heart shall resound like a harp for Moab, and my inner being for Kir Heres (Isaiah 16:11).

5. The Inward Parts

Behold, You desire truth in the inward parts, and in the hidden part You will make me to know wisdom (Psalm 51:6).

6. Our Inmost Parts

The words of a gossip are like choice morsels; they go down to a man's inmost parts (Proverbs 26:22 NIV).

7. The Inner Depths of the Heart

The spirit of a man is the lamp of the Lord, searching all the inner depths of his heart (Proverbs 20:27).

Blows that hurt cleanse away evil, as do stripes the inner depths of the heart (Proverbs 20:30).

Whichever way we look at it, the heart is arguably one of the most significant concepts in the entire Bible. God's creation of human beings is unquestionably the crowning achievement of His creative power and intelligent design because men and women are made in the very image and likeness of God. "Lord, what is man, that You take knowledge of him? Or the son of man, that You are mindful of him" (Psalm 144:3)?

According to the Scriptures, the eyes of God are intently focused upon the hearts of men. "The eyes of the Lord are everywhere, keeping watch on the wicked and the good" (Proverbs 15:3 NIV). "For the eyes of the Lord run to and fro throughout the whole earth to strengthen those whose hearts are fully committed to Him" (2 Chronicles 16:9). God is infinitely more concerned about the heart of just one of His children than He is about one thousand galaxies! We read in Job that God has literally set His heart on man. "What is man, that You should exalt him, that You should set Your heart on him" (Job 7:17)?

The *Dictionary of New Testament Theology* defines the heart as the seat of the "inner life in opposition to external appearance."[1] That's why God said to the prophet Samuel, "The Lord does not look at the things man looks at. Man looks at the outward appearance, but the Lord looks at the heart" (1 Samuel 16:7 NIV). Paul warned the church in Corinth about "those who boast in outward appearance rather than in what is in the heart" (2 Corinthians 5:12 RSV).

The American theologian, George Eldon Ladd, observed that the heart is the most important term used by Paul to describe the inner man. The Pauline usage is essentially the same as the Hebrew word *leb* and designates the inner life of man from various points of view. The heart or inner aspect of man is contrasted to the outward and visible.[2] Paul was simply developing the Old Testament teaching of the heart as that which stood in opposition to outward appearance. The Pharisees typified this preoccupation with outward appearance and the complete neglect of the true condition of their hearts. Jesus addressed the true state of their hearts when He said, "On the outside you appear to people as righteous but on the inside you are full of hypocrisy and wickedness" (Matthew 23:28).

The heart thus encompasses the whole inner person, and it is fitting to use the term because, like the physical heart, the spiritual heart is the very core of our being out of which all the issues of the inner life flow (Proverbs 4:23). Solomon wrote in the Book of Proverbs, "As in water face reflects face, so a man's heart reveals the man" (Proverbs 27:19). The heart is the central focus of God's dealings with man. God is not concerned with superficiality, but with getting to the heart of the matter. Whenever God speaks of the very core of His own being, He speaks of His heart. "Yes, I will rejoice over them to do them good... with all My heart and with all My soul" (Jeremiah 32:41).

Most often when the Scriptures speak of the heart of a person, they do so in order to reveal the true inner condition of that person. God passionately seeks the devotion of our whole heart. He calls you and me to turn to Him with *all your heart* (Joel 2:12), to believe in Him with *all your heart* (Acts 8:37), to search for Him with *all your heart* (Jeremiah 29:13), and to trust in Him with *all your heart* (Proverbs 3:5). "Whatever you do, work at it with *all your heart*, as working for the Lord, not for men" (Colossians 3:23).

As we saw in our introduction, it has often been said that the heart of man's problem is the problem of the heart. That is why the Scriptures exhort us to "Keep [our] heart with all diligence, for out of it spring the issues of life" (Proverbs 4:23). So we can say, in the light of the revelation of Scripture, that the heart is a broad-brush term used to describe the interior life of a person in contrast to the exterior or physical life of a person. It is the inward as opposed to the outward, which explains why God looks upon the heart.

The Heart and the Human Spirit

In the Bible we encounter highly specific language to describe the heart of man. These revelatory components are road-maps to the interior life. Without these revelatory concepts we would be completely clueless concerning the true nature of our interior life. Two terms in particular need to be defined as aspects of the heart: spirit and soul. Biblically, our heart encompasses both our spirit and our soul so we will endeavour to work toward a clear understanding of these two terms. The first term that describes an aspect of the inner man is the spirit. As a tripartite being (spirit, soul, and body) man possesses a spirit. This is what makes us *spiritual* beings. It is that part of us that constitutes our very life, which is why James taught, "The body without the spirit is dead" (James 2:26). We are spirit beings who live in a physical body. My spirit is the real me, and your spirit is the real you!

The spirit describes a unique aspect of the inner person of the heart. Prior to the advent of the new creation, the spirit and the heart were used interchangeably. In the Old Testament there was no theological distinction between the spirit and the heart because the fallen condition of man extended even to the defilement and corruption of the human spirit by sin. This is what necessitated the "new spirit" spoken of by the prophet Ezekiel. It is important that we distinguish between the old spirit and the new spirit. God said, "I will give you a new heart and put a *new spirit* within you" (Ezekiel 36:26). Let's take a look at how the Old Testament spoke of the fallen and defiled human spirit and the heart interchangeably.

In Proverbs we read, "All the ways of a man are pure in his own eyes but the Lord weighs the *spirits*" (Proverbs 16:2). Five chapters later we read, "Every way of a man is right in his own eyes but the Lord weighs the *hearts*" (21:2). We also read in Proverbs, "The *spirit* of a man is the lamp of the Lord, searching all the inner depths of his *heart*" (20:27). Frequently the spirit and the heart are used parallel with one another. Old Testament theologians call this Hebrew parallelism – a literary device that occurs throughout the Hebrew Scriptures. Let's carefully consider the way this parallelism is used in the following verses:

> Then everyone came whose heart was stirred, and everyone whose spirit was willing…They came, both men and women, as many as had a willing heart (Exodus 35:21-22).

> The sacrifices of God are a broken spirit, a broken and a contrite heart (Psalm 51:17).

> My spirit is overwhelmed within me; my heart within me is distressed (Psalm 143:4).

> I meditate within my heart, and my spirit makes diligent search (Psalm 77:6).

> By sorrow of the heart the spirit is broken (Proverbs 15:13).

> You shall cry for sorrow of heart, and wail for grief of spirit (Isaiah 65:14).

> For thus says the High and Lofty One who inhabits eternity, whose name is Holy: "I dwell in the high and holy place, with him who has a contrite and humble spirit, to *revive the spirit* of the humble, and to *revive the heart* of the contrite ones" (Isaiah 57:15).

Because human beings are understood holistically in the Bible, whatever condition their heart was in also defined the condition of their spirit. In the Old Testament all that could be said of the fallen condition of the heart could also be said of the spirit, as the following table indicates.

Steadfast spirit (Ps. 51:10)	Steadfast heart (Psalm 57:7; 112:7)
Faint spirit (Ez. 21:7)	Faint heart (Jer. 8:18)
Faithful spirit (Ps. 78:8)	Faithful heart (Neh. 9:8)
Hardened spirit (Deut. 2:30)	Hardened heart (Mark 6:52)
Overwhelmed spirit (Ps.143:4)	Overwhelmed heart (Ps. 61:2)
Failing spirit. (Ps. 143:7)	Failing heart (Ps. 40:12)
Broken spirit (Prov. 15:13, 17:22)	Broken heart (Ps. 34:8; 147:3)
Revived spirit (Isa. 57:15)	Revived heart (Isa. 57:15)
Grieved spirit (Isa. 65:14)	Grieved heart (1 Sam. 2:33)
Sorrowful spirit (1 Sam. 1:15)	Sorrowful heart (Ps. 13:2, 38:11)
Anguished spirit (Ex. 6:9)	Anguished heart (2 Cor. 2:4)
Troubled spirit (Gen. 41:8; John 13:21)	Troubled heart (John 14:1; Lam. 2:11)
Willing spirit (Ex. 35:21)	Willing heart (Ex. 35:5)
New spirit (Ez. 11:19)	New heart (Ez. 18:31; 36:26)

The Heart and the Soul

In the same way, all that can be said of the fallen condition of the heart can also be said of the soul. Every term used in the Scriptures to describe the various conditions of the human heart also adequately describe the condition of the soul. The following selection of Scriptures illustrates how the words heart and soul are used interchangeably.

> How long shall I take counsel in my *soul*, having sorrow in my *heart* daily (Psalm 13:2)?

> Who may ascend into the hill of the Lord? Or who may stand in His holy place? He who has clean hands and a pure *heart*, who has not lifted up his *soul* to an idol, nor sworn deceitfully (Psalm 24:3-4).

> My *soul* longs, yes, even faints for the courts of the Lord; my *heart* and my flesh cry out for the living God (Psalm 84:2).

The Knowledge of the Heart - Part One

> When wisdom enters your *heart,* and knowledge is pleasant to your *soul,* discretion will preserve you; understanding will keep you (Proverbs 2:10-11).

> O my soul, my soul! I am pained in my very heart! My heart makes a noise in me (Jeremiah 4:19).

> See, O Lord, that I am in distress; my soul is troubled; my heart is overturned within me (Lamentations 1:20).

> Now the multitude of those who believed were of one heart and one soul (Acts 4:32).

The Scriptures make no differentiation between pouring out our *soul* and pouring out our *heart* to God (see Psalm 42:4 and 62:8). Hannah was "in bitterness of soul" (1 Samuel 1:10), yet Solomon could say, "the heart knows its own bitterness" (Proverbs 14:10). If the heart is so intimately related to the soul, then why do the Scriptures differentiate between the two terms? Why does the term "all your heart and all your soul" appear approximately twenty times in the Bible if they essentially mean the same thing? For example, we are commanded in Deuteronomy to "love the Lord your God with all your heart, with all your soul, and with all your strength" (Deuteronomy 6:5). Even the Lord himself said in Jeremiah, "Yes, I will rejoice over them to do them good, and I will assuredly plant them in this land, with all My heart and with all My soul" (Jeremiah 32:41).

I think the answer to this question lies in the fact that the Bible clearly differentiates between soul and spirit yet includes these two concepts as an integral part of the heart. Let me explain. In the book of Hebrews we read, "The word of God is living and powerful, and sharper than any two-edged sword, piercing even to the division of soul and spirit, and of joints and marrow, and is a discerner of the thoughts and intents of the heart" (Hebrews 4:12).

This verse includes all three concepts of heart, soul, and spirit. This is an important New Testament theological differentiation. In the Old Testament there was a clear revelation of the tripartite nature of man. The language of heart, soul, and spirit is evident throughout all of the writings of the Old Testament. The line of demarcation only comes into sharp focus as a consequence of the new creation, which is a powerful New Covenant reality.

There is now a vital New Covenant imperative to differentiate between soul and spirit because of the new spirit that God has placed within every born again believer. In the Old Testament this human spirit was comprehensively defiled by sin and it was dead to God. But in the New Testament the human spirit is powerfully regenerated and renewed or made brand new. It is now gloriously alive to God and comprehensively purged of the defilement of sin. It has been made completely righteous in His sight.

Hence, there is a New Covenant imperative to thoroughly differentiate between the soul and the spirit. This differentiation only comes about through the revelation of the Word of God that divides soul from spirit. A further reason for the New Testament differentiation between soul and spirit is that the work that God has done in our regenerated spirit is a finished work—it cannot be improved upon—whereas, the work of God in our soul (our mind, will, and emotions) is an unfinished work. "He who began a good work in you will carry it on to completion until the day of Christ Jesus" (Philippians 1:6 NIV). We will explain this differentiation between soul and spirit in much greater detail in the next book, *The New Creation Miracle*.

This regeneration of the human spirit constitutes the foundation for the beginning of the transformation of the heart of the believer. Without this foundation set in place—through the new birth and through divine revelation—there cannot be any significant transformation in our lives. The work of the Holy Spirit in the New Covenant is to open our eyes to that which Ezekiel prophesied: God would put a "new spirit" within believers when the new creation dawned through the coming of the Messiah (see Ezekiel 37).

With this understanding of the biblical differentiation between the soul and the spirit, let's proceed to arrive at a clear definition of the soul and its relationship to the heart. The soul has traditionally been understood to comprise the mind, the will, and the emotions of a person. The heart therefore defines the very core of the mind, will, and emotions. As we will see as we progress through this series, it can be demonstrated from the Scriptures that there is a clearly defined theological relationship between the heart and the mind, the heart and the will, and the heart and the emotions. All three aspects of our soul are part of the interior life of the heart.

A theological investigation of these concepts illustrates precisely why the Scriptures delineate between the heart and the soul. This is an extremely important point because as we proceed to develop a biblical theology of the heart, we will see that when God speaks of the heart, He usually does so in direct reference to these three aspects of the soul. The Bible uses technically precise language when it comes to the theology of the heart. God wants us to take the time to get our theological definitions straightened out so that we can also use precise biblical language in seeking to define the interior dimensions of our being. We will further discuss this whole area of theological precision in greater detail toward the end of this book, but for now I want to make the point that we can arrive at solid biblical definitions of words used in the Old and New Testaments. It is helpful to clarify this point before we proceed any further.

So, in conclusion to our investigation into the question of what the Bible means by the term heart, we can conclude that our heart describes our interior life as opposed to our outward, physical life. Our heart includes our spirit. For the pre-Christian the spirit is dead to God and defiled by sin, but for the Christian our spirit has been gloriously renewed and made alive to God. It has also been comprehensively cleansed of sin and made righteous before God. Our heart also includes the three aspects of our soul: our mind, our will, and our emotions.

What Does the Bible Mean by the "Heart?"

I am always personally struck by the consistency of revelation in whatever subject I explore in the Scriptures. Whether I am studying the nature and attributes of God or the nature of fallen man, every book of the Bible contributes to our understanding of these powerful themes. Systematic theology is the systematizing of all of the theological themes of the Bible, and one of the greatest marvels of this process is the internal consistency of the Bible. The Bible is the only handbook and road-map of the human heart. There is no other! Without biblical revelation into the nature of the human heart and all of its components, we would be forever groping in the dark with endless speculations concerning the interior nature of our heart. God clearly wants us to know these things and to think biblically.

Chapter Three

The Lack of Heart Knowledge in the Church

My people are destroyed for lack of knowledge.
(Hosea 4:6)

Tom had been going to church for over fifteen years. He sometimes even conducted Bible studies in the home fellowship group that he and Jenny were a part of. But it was well known that his marriage was in tatters and that Jenny and the three children had lost all respect for him. Nothing ever seemed to change on the home front, except that Tom's kids had now entered the teenage years and his two eldest daughters were both sexually active. Tom had been through two separations with his wife and there had been plenty of discussion about the possibility of divorce. Their pain levels were now at an all-time high.

They had only been back together for four months when Jenny finally gave up. When Tom came home from work one day in July, Jenny had packed up all her treasured possessions and had simply walked out with the children. Tom quickly discovered that she had gone and he sunk into the couch, weeping bitterly over the devastation of his family. Christianity was supposed to make life better but Tom had known nothing but pain since the day he was married. Now his wife had left him for the third time and this time he knew for sure that his marriage was over.

God said through the prophet Hosea, "My people are destroyed for lack of knowledge" (Hosea 4:6). In light of this simple but powerful truth, it could well be argued that the church today is subtly being destroyed through a lack of knowledge of the true condition of the human heart and through a lack of knowledge of how to minister to the deepest problems that people face in life. Many Christians excel in many spheres of biblical knowledge but few excel in "heart knowledge." This prevailing trend amongst church-going believers is reflected in the reality that most Christians are right at home with an intellectually stimulating Bible study but they feel like fish out of water when it comes to confronting the deeper issues of their heart.

Why does there appear to be so little knowledge of the heart among Christians who are so familiar with the basic beliefs of Christianity? The truth is that we can acquire a thorough knowledge of almost any theological theme in the Bible without necessarily paying a high personal price. But a deep knowledge of the intricate contours of the heart simply cannot be attained without paying a high price in our personal lives. When God reveals the actual state of our heart, it always necessitates personal change, and that change is always extremely costly. Most Christians end up choosing to play it safe and focus their attention on subjects they can easily master. We are not at home with weakness and vulnerability because it makes us feel powerless.

Living in the twenty-first century affords us the luxury of twenty centuries of church history to survey in order to understand how the church has historically understood, or not understood, certain biblical truths. I completed a major in history in university back in the 1990s, and I have a personal passion for church history so I studied early church history, Reformation church history, the history of Christian missions, Australian church history, and a number of subjects in contemporary world history.

The Lack of Heart Knowledge in the Church

When we take a big picture view of church history as it relates to how the people of God have stewarded the fullness of the kingdom ministry of Jesus, it is always difficult to give an accurate overview. We recognise that God has always had a faithful remnant in almost every era of church history, but we can also see that there have been significant seasons of widespread apostasy from the true faith that Jesus handed to the church. Church history certainly is a diverse mixture.

For the purpose of this study we want to understand how the church has stewarded the message of the heart that Jesus pioneered two thousand years ago. Of course, in every age there have been Christians who have had a sincere desire to follow Jesus and to please God. These believers have had to deal with a number of heart issues just to survive in their relationship with God and other believers. There are entry-level heart issues that all Christians in every age must face because they are glaringly obvious to themselves and to others, especially when Jesus made love the universal standard of righteousness.

The issue of the call to the deep heart journey only becomes problematic when Christians are faced with the deeper issues of the heart that they don't understand, or when they cannot determine what they should do about the deeper strongholds of the heart. I believe the ultimate litmus test revolves around how Christians in ages past have dealt with the issue of healing the brokenhearted; this becomes a powerful lens through which to study church history. It is one thing to address issues of sin—and the church has always managed to give clear definition to the biblical admonition to "go and sin no more"—but the church's capacity to heal the broken-hearted and to minister to the real needs of deeply broken people becomes a measuring rod for the church's success or failure in the call to embrace the heart journey.

For centuries, much of the evangelical world has been largely absorbed with the pursuit of Christian doctrine. The evangelical concept of discipleship has usually focused almost exclusively upon training the intellect, rather than upon ministering to the deeper issues of the heart and the cultivation of a deep devotional life with God. This imbalance is plainly reflected in the curriculum of many theological colleges and seminaries. When someone responds to the call to ministry, they usually seek out further theological training but in too many Christian traditions, this training is almost exclusively focused upon the acquisition of theological information. Issues of the heart, in regard to our relationship to God and to one another, are generally relegated to the category of the devotional life. The result is that we have not done much theologizing about the heart, especially in our theological institutions.

Western Christianity has traditionally been weak in the area of cultivating the devotional life of the believer. For too many centuries, the evangelical tradition has been busy producing intellectual giants who are devotional pygmies. The theology of the heart is not even touched upon in many Christian traditions. Within many denominations the Christian faith has often been treated as a purely cerebral matter that revolves around the acquisition of specified theological information. In these circles, there seems to be a widespread disdain for the mystical stream of the church, with some evangelicals expressing outright contempt of mystically inclined believers. Yet it was the mystics who sought to preserve the core value of a deep heart engagement with the love of God. Whilst the mystic tradition had a number of weaknesses, they remained true to the paradigm of the divine romance between the bride and the Bridegroom.

But because the mystical stream of the church was significantly colored by a works-based theology, particularly in the Catholic tradition, the reformers used the mystics as examples of believers who shrugged off sound doctrine in favour of their own mystical encounters with God. This disdain of the mystic tradition has come to characterise many of the reformation streams of Western Christianity. In order to avoid the alleged errors of the mystics, reformation theologians sought to play it safe by sticking to sound doctrine, making this the focus of all ministerial training in the church.

This general trend is reflected in the reading material that is digested by many streams within the evangelical church. So much of the available literature is focused primarily upon issues of doctrinal precision whilst matters of the heart often tend to be marginalized. But we avoid the deeper issues of the heart to our own detriment. Conversion to Christ is meant to entail a conversion to living from the heart but, sadly, many new converts to Christ fall short in stepping into the fullness of true heart conversion. This error is strongly reinforced by theological training institutes that also seek to play it safe and avoid the alleged dangers of the mystical path.

The widespread absence of serious theological reflection upon the heart is a symptom of a far deeper problem. This problem is revealed in evangelicalism's systematic avoidance of the knowledge of the heart. If we are honest, we must acknowledge that the vast majority of Christians are far more comfortable thinking about anything other than the true state of their own heart. Is it any wonder so many Christians are being decimated and destroyed by the powers of darkness?

But there are some positive changes occurring within the church. More and more, Christians are being drawn to seek to understand how to find true freedom in Christ from the problems that deeply trouble people's lives. The church is slowly awakening to the realization of its historical imbalance and is slowly coming out of denial about the depth of human brokenness and our general lack of ministry experience in bringing authentic freedom to people's lives.

Some churches do genuinely seek to minister to the hurts and wounds of the broken-hearted, but many still prefer to leave this door permanently closed. As a general rule, those churches that acknowledge and discuss the reality of the deep emotional pain in the lives of its members and who seek to heal these deep wounds are the churches that are authentically wrestling with the issues of the heart that hinder our growth in intimacy. Although these churches are clearly in the minority, their presence within the broader evangelical community is a very encouraging sign.

The real problem is that many evangelicals have not done the hard work of developing a systematic theology of Christ's supernatural prophetic ministry to the heart. Meanwhile, the ancient biblical knowledge of the heart lies covered in dust like a musty antiquarian book that has not been removed from the bookshelf for centuries.

Because of the widespread absence of the knowledge of the heart, the church has also been stunted devotionally. We cannot grow in the devotional dimension of our Christian lives without coming to grips with the issues of the heart. All devotional growth hinges upon matters of the heart. Progress in the spiritual life cannot be attained without dealing with the deep issues of the hidden person of the heart in relation to God and our neighbor. This is why worship is so important to the growth of individual Christians. True worship that flows from the heart brings us in touch with those heart issues that would hinder us expressing our heart to God in sincerity and truth, rather than in pretence.

God is primarily concerned with the devotion and affections of the heart and with the cultivation of the interior life. The reality is that many evangelical Christians have an encyclopaedic knowledge of Scripture with almost no knowledge of the true condition of their own hearts or why their marriages are falling apart. Many years ago, I worked with a ministry colleague who had one of the sharpest theological minds I had ever encountered yet his marriage and his home life was in shambles. Eventually and predictably, his marriage fell apart because he absolutely refused to deal with the issues of the heart that were destroying his marriage.

Paul highlighted the imperative for the church to remain true to her calling of simple heartfelt devotion to Christ. The call to true intimacy is hotly contended by the powers of darkness. Paul said,

"But I am afraid that, as the serpent deceived Eve by his craftiness, your minds will be led astray from the simplicity and purity of devotion to Christ" (2 Corinthians 11:3 NASB). This powerful idea of simple heartfelt devotion to Christ is truly revolutionary. It speaks prophetically to those streams of the church that have determined, by their own volition, that theological information must be the currency of heaven.

But what if love has always been the currency? Paul's powerful juxtaposition between love and theological knowledge in his first epistle to the Corinthians certainly seems to establish this conviction. His opponents had made knowledge and theological information the new currency to which Paul replied, "We know that we all have knowledge. Knowledge puffs up, but love edifies and if anyone thinks that he knows anything, he knows nothing yet as he ought to know! But if anyone loves God, this one is known by Him" (1 Corinthians 8:1-3)!

There is an urgent need for the restoration of balance within the evangelical stream of the church. There is obviously a significant place for doctrinal teaching in the church today but this must be balanced by an equally strong emphasis upon the devotional life and matters of the heart. The church urgently needs to regain its position as "the head and not the tail" in offering leadership to the world in ministering to the real needs of broken and wounded people. This is what Jesus has always been looking for amongst His people.

In the book of Isaiah the Lord said that He would raise up reformers who would "rebuild the ancient ruins and restore the places long devastated; they will renew the ruined cities that have been devastated for generations" (Isaiah 61:4 NIV). There are ancient paths in the Scriptures that have, by and large, been neglected by Christians for generations. One of these paths may be found in the ancient knowledge of the heart concealed within the Scriptures and powerfully articulated by Jesus.

This is what the Lord says, "Stand at the crossroads and look; ask for the ancient paths, ask where the good way is, and walk in it, and you will find rest for your souls." But you said, "We will not walk in it" (Jeremiah 6:16).

We cannot begin to walk down this ancient path unless we are actually willing to let the Lord do the work of healing and restoration in our own hearts. It is a principle of the Scriptures that *knowing* only comes through *doing*. Jesus said, "Anyone who wants to do the will of God will know whether my teaching is from God or is merely my own" (John 7:17 NLT). We have to do the will of God in order to know it!

The doorway to an intimate knowledge of the heart comes, not through the accumulation of theological facts about the heart, but through allowing the Holy Spirit to illumine our hearts from the Scriptures and to allow the Word of God to accomplish that for which it has been sent, namely the radical transformation of the heart. It is only as God systematically transforms our hearts that our eyes are opened to the revelation of the ministry of the Holy Spirit to the human heart.

All true theology arises out of the impact of the Spirit of God upon the human heart. The best theologies are written as an immediate consequence of the personal assimilation of truth into the heart. The Scriptures were written by those who had been personally impacted by God, not by people who merely chose to pass on secondhand theological information. If we are willing to travel down this ancient path, we will indeed come to know the teaching, but only as we walk in the footsteps of the ancients who encountered God in personal mystical experience and experienced the powerful inner transformation of the heart.

One of the things God is seeking to do in this current wave of renewal that is sweeping the evangelical movement in the twenty first century is to restore to the church an understanding of the ministry of the Holy Spirit to the heart. In the process of this awakening, He is seeking to equip believers to become active participants with Him in ministering to the deepest issues of the hearts of men and women. Christians have a heritage of heart knowledge contained in the Scriptures that urgently needs to be recovered.

Hidden within the pages of Scripture is a body of revelation that radically outshines the most impressive secular speculations on the inner workings of human nature. But this dimension of spiritual revelation will remain completely hidden unless we choose to pursue the pathway of personal encounter with God. That is why some evangelicals have remained ignorant in the arena of the knowledge of the heart. This kind of spiritual knowledge only comes at the expense of the self-life.

The Charismatic renewal within the church is not an end in itself; it is merely a means unto an end. The ultimate goal of the Charismatic awakening is to bring the church into a deeper intimacy with God and to a radical transformation of the human heart. We cannot enter into true intimacy with the Father without embracing the reality of the prophetic nature of authentic New Testament Christianity. Jesus Christ is radically prophetic, and the heart of prophetic ministry is all about revealing the heart of God and the heart of man.

If we reject the reality of the prophetic, we cannot come to know God in the biblical sense of the term. He is the prophetic God who speaks, and when He speaks, He always speaks the language of the heart. As we personally come to experience the power of God to heal and restore our broken souls, we are equipped in the process to minister to others. We cannot minister to, or take our brothers and sisters beyond where we have gone ourselves. It is only as we learn to receive from God that we are equipped to give to those in spiritual need. This is the principle that Jesus was highlighting in his discussion about dealing with the plank in our own eye first.

> And why do you look at the speck in your brother's eye, but do not consider the plank in your own eye? Or how can you say to your brother, "Let me remove the speck from your eye," and look, a plank is in your own eye? Hypocrite! First remove the plank from your own eye, and then you will see clearly to remove the speck from your brother's eye (Matthew 7:3-5).

Paul highlighted this same principle of ministry in his second epistle to the Corinthians.

> Blessed be the God and Father of our Lord Jesus Christ, the Father of mercies and God of all comfort, who comforts us in all our tribulation that we may be able to comfort those who are in any trouble, with the comfort with which we ourselves are comforted by God (2 Corinthians 1:3-4).

If we have not personally experienced the comfort of the Lord in the midst of personal tribulation and suffering, we will not be able to effectively comfort or minister to others who are grieving or suffering. Similarly, if we have not opened up our own hearts to receive the ministry of the Holy Spirit, we will not be able to participate in the ministry of the Spirit in the lives of others.

But, on the other hand, when we have received something significant from the Lord, we suddenly find that we *are able to see clearly* and to understand what the Lord wants to do in other people's lives. Jesus said, "Freely you have received, freely give" (Matthew 10:8). The truth is that we can only give away that which we have first received from God. This is a New Testament principle of ministry. First, we allow the Lord to minister to us, and then we are in a position to give away what He has given to us.

This powerful principle of New Testament ministry explains the tragic deficit of heart knowledge that characterizes parts of the church in our day. Nobody enjoys having their personal world turned upside down as the Lord steps into our lives to expose the secret sins and the hidden wounds of the heart. Subsequently, many church members have chosen not to go down this path and as a result, they have remained largely unchanged.

In some instances, the intense warfare surrounding the church has caused some Christians to go backward rather than forward as long as they refuse to address the deeper issues of their hearts. The enemy of our souls rides on the back of un-confessed sin and emotional brokenness. So many Christians have settled for a cerebral Christianity that consists in the accumulation and regurgitation of biblical information. But this is not what Jesus had in mind for His people.

In thousands upon thousands of churches throughout the world, Christians go to church week after week and have their intellects stimulated by interesting spiritually oriented information, but the deeper issues of the heart are often left untouched. Of course there are numerous exceptions throughout the world where individual Christians or even individual churches have embraced this concept of "heart ministry" but it is true to say that, historically, the vast majority of evangelical churches have not substantially grown in this dimension of Christian experience.

God is in the process of triggering a powerful prophetic revolution to reform His church. He is passionately intentional about revealing the prophetic ministry of His Beloved Son. The Father is seeking to glorify the Son by openly revealing His ability to heal broken hearts and to deliver His people from sin and demonic influence. He is not content to have an expression of the church that does not adequately reflect the glorious ministry of Christ. He is seeking to fill the church with the fullness of Christ. This process begins with the people of God in every church under heaven opening their heart to the revelation of the ministry of Christ. As we press into this unfolding revelation of the glory of Christ, we will become a truly prophetic church that is well on its way to embracing the heart revolution that Jesus pioneered twenty centuries ago.

Chapter Four

Wisdom and the Knowledge of the Heart

Wisdom will enter your heart, and knowledge will be pleasant to your soul. Discretion will protect you, and understanding will guard you. Wisdom will save you from the ways of wicked men, from men whose words are perverse, who leave the straight paths to walk in dark ways, who delight in doing wrong and rejoice in the perverseness of evil, whose paths are crooked and who are devious in their ways.
(Proverbs 2:10-15)

Jack was raised in a loving Christian home but he rebelled against his parents and left home at an early age. This broke his parents' hearts, and they couldn't understand how he could have turned to crime when he had such a good upbringing. But his criminal activities were only the tip of the iceberg. Jack had become involved in robbery to fund a drug addiction, and his craving for heroin drove him to do a series crazy, reckless things.

At the age of nineteen, he ended up in prison because he walked into a shop with a gun and demanded all the money from the cash register. He ran out the door with only one hundred seventy-eight dollars, planning to jump into his car, which he had left outside with the engine running. But he ran straight into two police officers who were inspecting his abandoned car. It was hurriedly parked and the lights were left on. Jack was imprisoned for six months just before his twentieth birthday. When his dad came to see him at the police station, Jack hung his head in shame. He felt like the biggest fool; he couldn't even plan an intelligent robbery.

The Bible rather neatly divides humanity into two basic categories: the wise man and the fool. The fool is depicted as the person who has intentionally shut the knowledge of God out of his heart and who has rejected sound wisdom. The wisdom that the fool has rejected is the knowledge of the heart as it has been presented in the pages of Scripture. In my youth I immersed myself in the way of the fool, plunging into a narcissistic lifestyle of drugs, alcohol abuse, and immorality. I was fortunate to have met Christ at the age of nineteen, and I gingerly set out upon the way of wisdom but the legacy of my foolish ways lingered long into my journey as a follower of Jesus.

As I look back over the journey, I can still see so many threads of foolishness that have haunted me as a believer. Wisdom only comes to those who diligently pursue the knowledge of the heart. David said, "Teach us to number our days that we may present to You a heart of wisdom" (Psalm 90:12 NASB). Solomon prayed for a wise and understanding heart and God graciously led him in the way of true spiritual understanding. Solomon said, "Wisdom rests in the heart of him who has understanding but what is in the heart of fools is made known" (Proverbs 14:33).

When all that has been said concerning the heart in the Bible is gathered and systematized, it comprises a body of knowledge that is unsurpassed in its breadth of wisdom and insight into human nature. This body of divinely revealed information about the human condition can properly be called the knowledge of the heart. Not only does the Bible reveal an extraordinary depth of insight into the fallen condition of the human heart, it also reveals the nature of the heart of God. In this light, the Bible really is a tale of two hearts.

Wisdom and the Knowledge of the Heart

That which may be known and understood about the ways of God and the ways of man can properly be defined as a body of wisdom and understanding. Of course, the wisdom of God is multi-dimensional. There is the wisdom of leadership, government, finances, business, parenting, and human relationships. In fact, there is an expression of divine wisdom that applies to every sphere of human experience.

Whenever the Scriptures refer to wisdom, it is usually in direct relationship to knowledge and understanding. The wisdom of God is a divinely revealed knowledge; it comes only from God who graciously bestows wisdom upon all who humbly seek it. When wisdom enters the human heart, it makes us wise and understanding concerning the ways of the heart. The wisdom of God's Word deliberately juxtaposes the foolishness of the fallen human condition with the wisdom of the heart of God. Listen to the wise words of our Heavenly Father:

> My son, if you accept my words and store up my commands within you, turning your ear to wisdom and applying your heart to understanding, and if you call out for insight and cry aloud for understanding, and if you look for it as for silver and search for it as for hidden treasure, then you will understand the fear of the Lord and find the knowledge of God. For the Lord gives wisdom, and from His mouth comes knowledge and understanding. Then you will understand what is right and just and fair – every good path. For wisdom will enter your heart and knowledge will be pleasant to your soul. Discretion will protect you, and understanding will guard you. Wisdom will save you from the ways of wicked men, from men whose words are perverse, who leave the straight paths to walk in dark ways, who delight in doing wrong and rejoice in the perverseness of evil, whose paths are crooked and who are devious in their ways (Proverbs 2:1-15 NIV).

The book of Proverbs contains almost thirty references to the *ways* of the heart. Solomon did not claim to originate the words of wisdom

The Knowledge of the Heart - Part One

that he wrote. He described them as a revelation from heaven: something that was supernaturally revealed to his heart by God. Much of Solomon's wisdom, though it pertained to every sphere of human experience, focused on the condition of the heart. Solomon's journey into the knowledge of the heart began when he humbly asked the Lord for wisdom and knowledge on the day that he began to reign as king in Jerusalem.

> Solomon went up to the bronze altar before the Lord in the Tent of Meeting. That night God appeared to Solomon and said to him, "Ask for whatever you want me to give you." Solomon answered God, "You have shown great kindness to David my father and have made me king in his place. Now, Lord God, let your promise to my father David be confirmed, for you have made me king over a people who are as numerous as the dust of the earth. Give me wisdom and knowledge, that I may lead this people, for who is able to govern this great people of yours?" God said to Solomon, "Since this is your heart's desire and you have not asked for wealth, riches or honor, nor for the death of your enemies, and since you have not asked for a long life but for wisdom and knowledge to govern my people over whom I have made you king, therefore wisdom and knowledge will be given you" (2 Chronicles 1:6-12).

God gave Solomon wisdom and very great insight, and a breadth of understanding as measureless as the sand on the seashore. Solomon's wisdom was greater than the wisdom of all the men of the East, and greater than all the wisdom of Egypt. He was wiser than any other man, and his fame spread to all the surrounding nations. He spoke three thousand proverbs and his songs numbered a thousand and five. Men of all nations came to listen to Solomon's wisdom, sent by all the kings of the world, who had heard of his wisdom (1 Kings 4:29-34).

Wisdom and the Knowledge of the Heart

King Solomon received this wisdom and knowledge directly from the Lord as he walked out his life before the Lord. God gave Solomon a depth of wisdom and insight into human nature that was unsurpassed. The primary focus of that wisdom and knowledge was an intimate knowledge of the ways of the human heart. As God progressively enlightened Solomon, he came to realize the folly of the hearts of men as they sought to live independently from God.

Solomon wrote the entire book of Proverbs as a revelation from God about the human heart. There can be no doubt that for Solomon, wisdom was centred in the knowledge of the heart. The book of Proverbs contains almost ninety references to the heart (NKJV) whilst Ecclesiastes, also written by Solomon, contains an additional forty references. These two books constitute almost ten percent of the references to the heart in the entire Bible! That ought to tell us something about the theme of Solomon's writings.

Proverbs contrasts the heart of the fool with the heart of the wise and enlightened man who has received the knowledge of God. "The lips of the wise spread knowledge; not so the hearts of fools" (Proverbs 15:7 NIV). What is wisdom? It could be defined as the virtue of applying revelatory knowledge with common sense and insight. It could also be defined as an accumulated state of spiritual enlightenment. For Solomon, wisdom came through his lifelong observation of the graphic contrast between the wisdom of the heart of God and the foolishness of the hearts of fallen men. The pursuit of wisdom as it pertained to the heart of man became Solomon's great obsession.

> I set my mind to seek and explore by wisdom concerning all that has been done under heaven. I have seen all the works that have been done under the sun, and behold, all is vanity and striving after the wind. What is crooked cannot be straightened and what is lacking cannot be counted. I said to myself, "Behold, I have magnified and increased in wisdom more than all who were over Jerusalem before me; and my

mind has observed a wealth of wisdom and knowledge." I set my mind to know wisdom and to know madness and folly... in much wisdom there is much grief, and increasing knowledge results in increasing pain (Ecclesiastes 1:13-18).

As Solomon grew in wisdom and knowledge, he came to realize that the more God revealed to him about the true condition of the human heart the more it produced a deepening sense of grief and pain within his own being. Because the heart of the fool prefers ignorance about the knowledge of his true spiritual condition, he is left to wallow in his folly. "A fool finds no pleasure in understanding" (Proverbs 18:2 NIV). "Fools despise wisdom and instruction" (Proverbs 1:7).

Solomon embarked on a journey of the knowledge of the heart but it was the road less travelled and he had very few companions. The price he paid for his depth of spiritual insight was grief and pain, and he learned that precious few were willing to step outside the comfort zone of blissful ignorance. Through his quest for wisdom and knowledge, Solomon concluded that "most men will proclaim each his own goodness" (Proverbs 20:6) rather than embrace the painful truth about the human condition. It is the fool who despises the knowledge of the ways of the heart. A fool remains a fool purely because he rejects the wisdom of God. Every aspect of his life subsequently reveals this deficit of divine wisdom.

Solomon came to recognise that most people reject the knowledge of the heart because they are too attached to the pursuit of personal pleasure. "The heart of the wise is in the house of mourning, but the heart of fools is in the house of pleasure" (Ecclesiastes 7:4 NIV).

In the light of everything that God had revealed to him concerning the true condition of the human heart, Solomon concluded that it was absolute madness to reject the wisdom of God. "Truly the hearts of the sons of men are full of evil; madness is in their hearts while they live" (Ecclesiastes 9:3).

Wisdom and the Knowledge of the Heart

Solomon's road less travelled revealed to him that "The fear of the Lord is the beginning of wisdom, and the knowledge of the Holy One is understanding" (Proverbs 9:10 NIV). He was endowed with such great wisdom and knowledge because he revered the Lord and he came to the same revelation that John the Baptist so clearly articulated: "A man can receive nothing unless it has been given to him from heaven" (John 3:27). It takes a step of genuine humility to embrace God's wisdom, and until a person takes that first step, they will remain a fool. James called it "the wisdom that is from above" (James 3:17).

Solomon understood that divine wisdom only settles upon the hearts of those who humble themselves before the Lord and who acknowledge that the greatest human wisdom is pure folly in the sight of God. "The wisdom and knowledge that comes from above is hidden from the wise and prudent of this world and it is revealed to babes; to those who become like little children and who are willing to sit at the feet of the Master and to allow Him to shine His light into the darkened recesses of the human heart" (Matthew 11:25).

Solomon drew many conclusions in his pursuit of wisdom but perhaps the greatest lesson was the revelation that if we would succeed in life, we must become people of the heart. The man or woman who is instructed in prophetic revelation will become wise beyond his or her years. They will have penetrating prophetic insight into the ways of the heart. It is the essence of divine wisdom to share this common insight of the Lord into the ways of the heart. The Lord imparts spiritual wisdom to all who seek it so that we begin to view all of life through the eyes of God. If we will become the friends of God, we will share with Jesus this capacity to see into the human heart; we will know how to minister to the deepest spiritual needs of those whose lives intersect with our own.

Solomon's wisdom was eclipsed only by the wisdom of Jesus. Jesus Himself honoured the extraordinary wisdom of Solomon by saying,

"The queen of Sheba ... came from a distant land to hear the wisdom of Solomon. And now someone greater than Solomon is here – and you refuse to listen to Him" (Luke 11:31 NLT). Everything Solomon received, he received directly from Jesus who is described in the New Testament as the very personification of the "wisdom of God" (see 1 Corinthians 1:24).

Solomon had a penetrating insight into human nature but Jesus could see even more deeply into the heart of every person He encountered, simply because He intimately knew the heart of His Father. At the very outset of Jesus' earthly ministry we read, "Many believed in His name when they saw the signs that He did. But Jesus did not commit Himself to them, because He knew all men... for He knew what was in man" (John 2:23-25). The New Living Translation says that Jesus "knew what people were really like. No one needed to tell him about human nature."

Jesus demonstrated a penetrating insight into human nature. He always spoke directly to the issues of the heart. That is why Jesus declined the opportunity to commit Himself to the rabble. He was waiting on the Father to show Him the specific people to whom He should commit Himself. He refused to invest Himself in people who would casually discard His wisdom. He refused to "cast His pearls before swine." Jesus sought faithful men and women of integrity who would hear His words and treasure them in their hearts.

It would have been a waste of time for Jesus to spend His limited sojourn on earth in the continuous company of fools who despised the Spirit of wisdom and revelation. Instead, Jesus sought out disciples who would receive an impartation of wisdom into the ways of the heart and employ this wisdom in the ministry of the kingdom of God.

If Solomon made disciples, it would have been his priority to impart his great wisdom to those who would sit at his feet. But it is not clear that Solomon ever made any disciples. But Jesus was sent into the world with a specific mandate to make disciples. It was His mission to invest the fullness of His divine wisdom into trustworthy disciples who would be skilled in ministering to the real needs of the human heart, just as Jesus modelled in His earthly ministry.

Jesus said to the religious leaders of Israel, "Therefore I am sending you prophets and wise men and teachers" (Matthew 23:34). Jesus, the ultimate prophet, spent three years raising up a company of prophets who could speak to the deepest issues of the human heart. How does God measure the nature of a true disciple of Christ? Jesus taught that the essence of true discipleship was to become just like our Divine Teacher. "It is enough for the disciple that he becomes like his Teacher" (Matthew 10:25). Jesus could send forth a company of "wise men" because they had walked with the Master and had become truly wise.

Perhaps it would be helpful for contemporary Christians to rethink the true nature of Christian discipleship. If Jesus was bestowed with a penetrating prophetic insight into the ways of the human heart, shouldn't it be the goal of every true follower of Jesus to be similarly endowed? The emergence of a vast company of prophets and wise men and women who had an unparalleled insight into human nature and who were equipped with the skills to minister to the deepest needs of the human heart would certainly be a phenomena in the midst of a church that so often fails to distinguish itself from the world in its chronic inability to escape the folly of living in bondage to the flesh.

It is my dream that every true follower of Christ will embrace the calling to minister just as Jesus ministered. To achieve this goal we must welcome the impartation of the prophetic knowledge of the heart. We must sit at the feet of Jesus and receive His instruction until we are overflowing with prophetic insight and wisdom into the ways of the heart. Then we will see a church emerge that will be gifted with the wisdom and power to bring significant transformation to the lives of everyone to whom we minister. Then we will start to become like our Teacher in His great wisdom and understanding.

James said, "If any of you lacks wisdom, let him ask of God, who gives to all generously and without reproach, and it will be given to him" (James 1:5). Are you willing to become one of the prophets and wise men that God is sending out into the world? Jesus worked with His disciples for three years, continually addressing their heart issues and training them to live from the heart. There is a price tag for this kind of wisdom and it only comes through embracing the heart journey. The knowledge of the heart is worth more than gold or silver; it is worth selling everything in order to obtain.

Jesus came to start a revolution. He introduced His disciples to an entirely new way of living that was built on the foundation of wisdom and glory. He trained them to walk in wisdom by continually bringing them in touch with what was going on inside their hearts until they were fully converted to living from the heart. This was the number one core value that Jesus instilled into this emerging company of prophets and wise men. The disciples had the ultimate privilege of walking with Wisdom incarnate, and the legacy of Jesus' method of discipleship has been left for the entire world to see. This handful of men changed the world and continued the glorious kingdom ministry of Jesus with tremendous fruitfulness.

The disciples turned a massive corner because they intentionally adopted the way of wisdom. Jesus made an interesting comment concerning this heavenly path of wisdom. He said, "Wisdom is justified by her children" (Luke 7:35). This essentially means that the way of wisdom is vindicated by those who embrace it. The New Living Translation says, "Wisdom is shown to be right by the lives of those who follow it." What is the outcome of our ways? Wisdom produces a heart that knows God intimately and can show others the way of wisdom.

The Lord said to Solomon, "See, I have given you a wise and understanding heart, so that there has not been anyone like you" (1 Kings 3:12). The impartation of divine wisdom makes you a standout person. Wisdom ushers you into the company of kings. Job said, "God is wise in heart and mighty in strength" (Job 9:4). God says, "My son, if your heart is wise, My own heart also will be glad; and my inmost being will rejoice when your lips speak what is right" (Proverbs 23:15-16 NASB). If we desire to be numbered amongst that company whom heaven calls "prophets and wise men" we need to get on board with the heart revolution, because this is Jesus' way of transforming the world.

Wisdom is vindicated by its outcome. This is a secret revolution of the heart in the way we carry ourselves before God and man. This revolution was quietly underway in the hearts of a few ordinary men but was subsequently revealed for the entire world to see just three short years later. Acts 4:13 says, "Now when they saw the boldness of Peter and John, and perceived that they were uneducated and untrained men, they marvelled. And they realized that they had been with Jesus." Proximity to Jesus is the key! If we truly walk with Jesus we will also become wise in heart, and we will live in the knowledge and understanding of the heart.

Those early apostolic leaders who "turned the world upside down" (Acts 17:6) could move in such high levels of wisdom and power because they had been immersed into the very culture of heaven for three years. Jesus carried the rarefied atmosphere of heaven and His disciples lived continually in that atmosphere as they walked, talked, and ministered with Jesus. Their hearts were excessively exposed to high levels of the divine glory that radiated out of Jesus.

They lived in the presence of the supernatural power of God for three whole years, continually witnessing the raw power of God to heal thousands of sick people and to cast out thousands of demons. They were intentionally discipled and trained by God incarnate so they had the best Mentor in the universe. They lived in the presence of the pure, unconditional love of God continually. All of this exposure would have to do something incredible inside your heart! Jesus taught them how to have a heart relationship with the Father and how to prioritize their heart journey of ever deepening intimacy.

Contemporary Christians often miss out on all of these essential elements so it is no great surprise that we are not seeing millions of great prophets and wise men emerging. Continual exposure to God is the incubator of prophets and wise men. If we want to produce the same outcome as Jesus, we need all of these essential elements restored to the church. At the centre of this is the recovery of apostolic wisdom and power to mentor the next generation of believers to a place where they are on the same page with Jesus and His agenda to transform hearts and lives through exposure to the culture of heaven.

Jesus built community around Him by calling a company of men and women into intimate relationship and by immersing them into the glory realm of heaven. He understood that only a life of full immersion would achieve the results that He was seeking.

Chapter Five

Kardiognostes:

Only God Knows the Heart

> Even the depths of Death and Destruction are known by
> the Lord. How much more does He know the human heart?
> (Proverbs 15:11 NLT)

Bob sat there in the chair, staring off into the distance. The expression on his wife's face revealed that she was growing increasingly frustrated. "How does this situation make you feel Wendy?" the counsellor inquired.

Wendy replied, "I can't stand it when he goes quiet like this. I just want him to talk and express how he really feels. But he never talks!"

"How are you feeling right now Bob?" The marriage counsellor probed Bob for a response but he sat there like a deer caught in the headlights.

He was obviously uncomfortable with this line of questioning and all he could do was shrug and repeat the phrase that was causing his wife to feel like giving up altogether on the marriage, "I don't know really."

How many marriage counselling situations have hit this impasse, where one or both parties are incapable of articulating the deepest feelings of their heart? Usually it is the husband.

We are often deeply aware that we have problems in our relationships yet fail to find the source of the problem. "The purposes of a man's heart are deep waters, but a man of understanding draws them out" (Proverbs 20:5 NIV). One of the greatest skills of a counsellor (or a man or woman of understanding) is the ability to probe the deep places of the heart and to draw out the issues that have caused the impasse. Only then can the couple identify the root of the problem and begin to move forward to resolve the impasse.

Why would Solomon describe the purposes of a man's heart as *deep waters?* Well, the problem with deep waters is that you cannot see the bottom. At some point, as a diver goes deeper and deeper into the ocean, the light fails to penetrate any further. What lies beneath becomes dark and mysterious. Without the aid of another light source, those things that lie at the bottom of the ocean will never come to the light.

Only God fully knows the human heart. From Genesis to Revelation it is clear that apart from divine revelation we are completely cut off from the *means* of knowing the true condition of our own heart. Jesus is the consummate "man of understanding," and He has come specifically to reveal the sinful and broken heart of humanity in order that those who are lost might come to repentance and salvation. Only a man or woman of prophetic understanding can draw out that which is hidden.

In fact, if we were to try to define the exact nature of the ministry of Jesus, we could effectively say that He came to unveil people's hearts and to reveal the heart of God toward broken people. Without this initial unveiling of the fallen condition of our hearts, we cannot be saved. Once we have come into the kingdom of God, we need to adjust our spiritual eyes to the light, just like a person who has emerged from years of living in the deep darkness of some subterranean cavern. Learning to live in the light means that we are learning to live in an intimate relationship with God who sees into the depths of our heart. God loves us even in those times when He sees us still living in bondage to sin and selfishness.

The Hidden Person of the Heart

As we have already seen, the Apostle Peter spoke about what he called the "hidden person of the heart" (1 Peter 3:4). Paul spoke of the "inner man" (Ephesians 3:16) or the "inward man" (2 Corinthians 4:16), and both of these ideas correspond to Peter's concept of the hidden person of the heart. This hidden person is the true inner person who needs to be distinguished from any false perception we may have generated about ourselves, or which we may have projected upon others. It is not a matter of whom we wish we were, but who we are in reality. This is the person that God sees when He looks into our hearts.

The Greek word used by Peter for hidden is *kruptos*. This word means *concealed, private, or secret*. Peter chose this particular word under the inspiration of the Holy Spirit to indicate that the true condition of the heart is entirely hidden or concealed. Paul used the same Greek word in 1 Corinthians 14:25 when he spoke of the *secrets* of the heart. He also used the word *kruptos* when he said that God "will bring to light what is *hidden* in darkness and will expose the motives of men's hearts" (1 Corinthians 4:5 NIV). The language of the Scriptures points us to the fact that, unaided by divine revelation, we are incapable of discovering or knowing the true condition of our hearts. We are entirely dependent on God for this knowledge.

Under the inspiration of the Holy Spirit, Jeremiah stated, "The heart is deceitful above all things and desperately wicked; *who can know it?*" (Jeremiah 17:9). This verse states emphatically that no one, without the assistance of divine revelation, can come to an accurate knowledge of his or her own heart. Immediately following this verse, Jeremiah wrote, "I the Lord search the heart, I test the mind, even to give every man according to his ways, and according to the fruit of his doings" (Jeremiah 17:10). This is what God sees when He looks into the heart of an unbeliever.

God searches the heart and He tests the mind. The Hebrew word for mind is *kelayot,* which means *the kidneys* in ancient Hebrew. Colin

Brown, the author of the *Dictionary of New Testament Theology*, tells us that the *kelayot* are "frequently mentioned in close connection to the heart. They are, in a metaphorical sense, the seat of the deepest spiritual emotions and motives, so secret that men cannot fathom them. Only God is able to search and test them."[3]

David used this same word *kelayot* in one of his prayers: "Test me O Lord and try me, examine my heart and my *mind*" (Psalm 26:2). Jesus said, "All the churches shall know that I am He who searches the minds and hearts" (Revelation 2:23). The Greek word used for m*inds* in this verse is *nephros*, which also means the *kidneys*. This Greek word corresponds exactly to the Hebrew word *kelayot* and it is used metaphorically to describe the deepest spiritual motives of a person's innermost being.

As we have already seen, it is the Lord's purpose to "bring to light what is hidden in darkness and [to] expose the motives of men's hearts" (1 Corinthians 4:5). Jesus is claiming that He is the One who searches the deepest motives of the human heart. He is the One who spoke in Jeremiah 17:10 that no one can know the depths of the human heart except God. In Jeremiah 17:9, God searches the heart of the unbeliever but in Revelation 2:23, He searches the heart of the believer.

We read earlier in the book of Hebrews that "Nothing in all creation is hidden from God's sight. Everything is uncovered and laid bare before the eyes of him to whom we must give account" (Hebrews 4:13). In Proverbs we read, "Even the depths of Death and Destruction are known by the Lord. How much more does He know the human heart?" (Proverbs 15:11 NLT). David was contemplating the awesome omniscience of God in Psalm 139 when he said,

> O Lord, You have searched me and known me. You know my sitting down and my rising up; You understand my thoughts afar off. You comprehend my path and my lying down, and are acquainted with all my ways. For there is not a word on

my tongue, but behold, O Lord, You know it altogether. You have hedged me behind and before, and laid Your hand upon me. Such knowledge is too wonderful for me; it is high, I cannot attain it (Psalm 139:1-6).

While we may find the omniscience of God unfathomable to our finite minds, we are faced with the reality that God knows everything about us: every single detail, thought, hidden attitude and motive behind our actions. Jesus said, "The very hairs of your head are all numbered" (Matthew 10:30). Such knowledge is indeed beyond us, but on every page of Scripture we are confronted with the truth of a God who numbers every grain of sand and every star in the sky. In the light of this revelation, David exclaimed, "Such knowledge is too wonderful for me!" (Psalm 139:6). It is truly breathtaking!

In the book of Acts, Luke describes God's comprehensive knowledge of the human heart by using a Greek word not used anywhere else in the Bible. The first time this word is recorded, it was on the lips of the eleven Apostles as they sought to determine a replacement for Judas, who had committed suicide. "And they prayed and said, "You, O Lord, who know the hearts of all, show which of these two You have chosen" (Acts 1:24).

The word that Luke used to describe this aspect of God's omniscience was *kardiognostes*, which means the knowledge of the heart. In this context it appears to have been used as a divine title: God is the Knower of Hearts. Peter, who reported the outpouring of the Holy Spirit upon the Gentiles, also used the same Greek word kardiognostes. "God, who knows the heart, showed that He accepted them by giving the Holy Spirit to them, just as He did to us" (Acts 15:8 NIV).

This all-knowing God, who intimately searches our hearts and minds, does not look at people the way we do. Many of us would remember the words to Samuel the prophet on that remarkable day he came to the house of Jesse to anoint David as King over Israel:

"Do not look at his appearance or at the height of his stature, because I have refused him. For the Lord does not see as man sees; for man looks at the outward appearance, but the Lord looks at the heart" (1 Samuel 16:7).

God consistently looks beyond outward appearances and looks deep into our hearts. Jesus spoke this discomforting reminder to the Pharisees, "You are those who justify yourselves before men, but God knows your hearts" (Luke 16:15). The outward religion of the Pharisees might have convinced those around them, but it didn't convince the Lord. God could look straight into their hearts and see through the walls of religious pretence. Remember the words of the psalmist: "If we had forgotten the name of our God ... would not God search this out? For He knows the secrets of the heart" (Psalm 44:21). In similar fashion, Solomon wrote in the book of Proverbs, "The lamp of the Lord searches the spirit of a man; it searches out his inmost being" (Proverbs 20:27 NIV). Or, as the New King James Version translates it, the Lamp of the Lord searches "all the inner depths of his heart."

For Solomon, the penetrating gaze of God into the human heart was one of the fundamental principles of divine revelation. On the day of the dedication of Solomon's temple, he prayed to God saying, "Forgive, and deal with each man according to all he does, since you know his heart: for you alone know the hearts of men" (2 Chronicles 6:30). David said to Solomon just before he died, "And you, my son Solomon, acknowledge the God of your father, and serve Him with wholehearted devotion and with a willing mind, for the Lord searches every heart and understands every motive behind the thoughts" (1 Chronicles 28:9 NIV). The hidden motives behind our thoughts and our actions are extremely important to God. He always perceives what motivates our behavior, even when we cannot.

It would seem that the entire foundation of David and Solomon's thoughts orbited around this fact of infinite divine omniscience. The book of Proverbs is an encyclopaedia of these kinds of profound insights into God's knowledge of the human heart. Solomon was trained by the Holy Spirit to look beyond outward human appearance to the deeper issues of the heart. "All a man's ways seem innocent to him, but motives are weighed by the Lord" (Proverbs 16:2). The more I meditate upon the Scriptures, the more this immovable fact becomes the rock to which my life is anchored: God knows my heart and He searches my deepest motives. And even when He sees me still stuck in my brokenness, He unconditionally loves me!

The Veiled Heart

The writers of the New Testament never minced words. They tell us quite bluntly that the whole of fallen humanity inhabits a realm of spiritual darkness and that people are quite content to stay there because they innately fear and despise the light. But why do human beings habitually avoid the light and cling to the shadows? The answer lies in the fact that in our fallen state we inwardly deplore the light because it exposes what is really in our hearts. It confirms our deepest fears about ourselves. It exposes those things that we work so hard to keep concealed because we fear that others might see our flaws and reject us. Shame and the fear of rejection are two motivations that drive people deep into the shadows.

Jesus said, "This is the condemnation, that the light has come into the world, and men loved darkness rather than light, because their deeds were evil. For everyone practicing evil *hates the light* and does not come to the light, lest his deeds should be exposed" (John 3:19-20). Exposure means anguish and pain, and humans habitually avoid emotional pain at all costs. Exposure also creates a heightened sense of helplessness, because most people reach a point where their personal problems become unmanageable. Often, facing those problems makes people feel dis-empowered. And since no one deliberately desires to feel dis-empowered, this increases people's motivation to avoid the light. We love to feel that we are in full control.

Paul taught that a veil lies over the heart of every unbeliever. This veil prevents the light of God from penetrating their hearts. "A veil lies on their heart. Nevertheless, when one turns to the Lord, the veil is taken away" (2 Corinthians 3:15-16). Some people deliberately choose the veil of darkness to keep the light out; they reach out for it like the cord on the window blind. They habitually pull down the shutters because they don't want to see what is in them.

The only thing that removes this veil is repentance. The Greek word for v*eil* is *kaluma*, which is a derivative of the Greek word *kalupto*. This Greek word is actually related to *kruptos*, which means "concealed, hidden, or secret." That which is veiled is hidden or concealed. Do you remember our discussion on the hidden person of the heart? *Kalupto* is the antonym of *apokalupto* from which we derive the English word apocalyptic or apocalypse.

Whenever we hear this word, we automatically associate it with the book of Revelation and the end of the world, but *apokalupto* actually means to reveal or to unveil. This significant Greek word describes the removal of the veil. Christians are well acquainted with the word revelation. This little lesson from the Greek language indicates that the only solution to the veil that covers the human heart is the revelation or unveiling of the heart. And the only thing that paves the way for the light of revelation to penetrate the inner depths of the heart is a voluntary choice to repent before God. So when someone "turns to the Lord" in genuine repentance, the veil is removed.

Jesus deliberately unveiled and exposed the wickedness of the fallen heart in order to call mankind to radical repentance. He said, "I have not come to call the righteous, but sinners, to repentance" (Luke 5:32). Jesus' first word recorded in the Gospel of Mark was, "The time is fulfilled, and the kingdom of God is at hand. *Repent*, and believe in the gospel" (Mark 1:15). On another occasion he said, "I tell you ... unless you repent you will all likewise perish" (Luke 13:5). Matthew 11:20 tells us, "Then He began to rebuke the cities in which most of His mighty works had been done, because they did not repent."

Jesus' ministry always focused upon the actual condition of the human heart. He was on a mission to expose sin in the human heart in order to promote repentance leading to salvation. Because this was His mission, He spoke the language of "exposing that which had been hidden." He said, "There is nothing covered that will not be revealed, and hidden that will not be known" (Matthew 10:26). Jesus relentlessly exposed both the heart condition of the Pharisees and the hard-heartedness of His own disciples. "Jesus said to them, 'Do you not yet perceive nor understand? Is your heart still hardened'" (Mark 8:17)?

It must have been incredibly challenging to walk with Jesus on earth, because He didn't give His disciples much room to indulge in their old sinful nature. "Later He appeared to the eleven as they sat at the table; and He rebuked their unbelief and hardness of heart, because they did not believe those who had seen Him after He had risen" (Mark 16:14). On another occasion after His resurrection, He said to the disciples, "Why are you troubled? And why do doubts arise in your hearts?" (Luke 24:38). Jesus spoke directly to the condition of the heart on every occasion. He just refused to do superficiality. This is why the disciples were tempted to turn back on so many occasions.

The entire prophetic testimony of the Old Testament is that man is self-deceived concerning his true condition. Prophet after prophet denounced the sinful and hypocritical hearts of the people of God, and Jesus was the consummate prophet in this historical prophetic tradition. His death was inevitable. Indeed, as story after story in the Gospels revealed, it was amazing that Jesus ministered for as long as He did, given the amount of satanically inspired opposition that He generated!

When we talk about the Word of God judging the hidden thoughts and motives of the heart, we need look no further than the ministry of Jesus—the Word of God incarnate—to behold the extraordinary impact that the Word has upon the human heart. His words "cut to the heart" and caused the hearts of His disciples to "burn within them." His words were like a sharp two-edged sword that proceeded out of His mouth. And as all who came in contact with Him could testify: the Word of God pierced their heart like a sword. Do you remember Simeon's prophecy to Mary in the temple? "This child is destined to cause the falling and rising of many in Israel, and to be a sign that will be spoken against, so that the thoughts of many hearts will be revealed. And a sword will pierce your own soul too" (Luke 2:34-35 NIV). The Sword of the Spirit reveals the secrets of the heart.

The Pharisees bore the brunt of this sharp sword because they had embraced certain biblical truths intellectually but they did not allow the Word of God to really penetrate and convict their hearts. Pharisees such as Nicodemus were rare, because he allowed the Word of God to convict him and promote repentance. As the psalmist came to understand, "Behold, You desire truth in the inward parts, and in the hidden parts You will make me to know wisdom" (Psalm 51:6). It has always been God's intention for His word to penetrate like a sword deep into the heart, not just the intellect. He said to Ezekiel, "Son of man, let all My words sink deep into your own heart first. Listen to them carefully for yourself" (Ezekiel 3:10 NLT). Everyone who engages with the Scriptures needs to beware of the power of religion that makes us so familiar with the Word of the Lord that we fail to allow it to cut to the heart.

Unveiling the Heart of the Unbeliever

The process by which we come to a true understanding of the hidden person of the heart is through the unveiling of the heart by the revelatory agency of the Holy Spirit. Paul explained the actual mechanics of this process in his writings; he was keenly aware of the power of the Word of God to bring enlightenment once the veil is removed. He spoke in terms of the "eyes of our heart being enlightened" (Ephesians 1:18). Prior to this experience, we are spiritually blind. The Greek word Paul used for *enlightened* was *photizo,* which speaks of light penetrating the veil over our hearts with the result that we begin to see the actual condition of our heart. The *New Living Translation* renders this verse in this way: "I pray that your hearts will be flooded with light...."

Prior to this enlightenment experience, we are completely blinded to the true condition of our hearts. Paul said it this way, "The god of this age has blinded the minds of unbelievers, so that they cannot see the light of the gospel of the glory of Christ, who is the image of God" (2 Corinthians 4:4 NIV). According to Paul, when we are enlightened by the work of the Holy Spirit, the light of God actually penetrates the heart. "For it is the God who commanded light to shine out of darkness, *who has shone into our hearts* to give the light of the knowledge of the glory of God in the face of Jesus Christ" (2 Corinthians 4:6).

Only the light of God can penetrate and remove this veil that covers the heart of every man and woman. But when the light of God penetrates the heart we come to a sudden realization that we are sinful and have offended a holy God. This revelation of the sinfulness of the fallen human heart is a prerequisite for salvation. In fact, we will not turn to God in repentance as long as we persist in the delusion that we are essentially good by nature. Solomon had a lot to say about this delusional state. He tells us "most men proclaim each his own goodness" (Proverbs 20:6). Without this *photizo* experience we can actually believe that about ourselves. Apart from this light that comes from God, it seems to be a universal problem that people seek to convince themselves that they are actually pure and righteous. "All the ways of a man are pure in his own eyes, but motives are weighed by the Lord" (Proverbs 16:2). "There is a generation that is pure in its own eyes yet is not washed from its filthiness" (Proverbs 30:12). The Bible calls this condition self-righteousness, and it can only flourish in dark places where the Spirit of revelation is unwelcome. Jesus tells the parable of the delusional state of the self-righteous Pharisee:

To some who were *confident of their own righteousness* and looked down on everybody else, Jesus told this parable: "Two men went up to the temple to pray, one a Pharisee and the other a tax collector. The Pharisee stood up and prayed about himself: 'God, I thank you that I am not like other men – robbers, evildoers, adulterers – or even like this tax collector. I fast twice a week and give a tenth of all I get.' But the tax collector stood at a distance. He would not even look up to heaven, but beat his breast and said, 'God, have mercy on me, a sinner.' I tell you that this man, rather than the other, went home justified before God. For everyone who exalts himself will be humbled, and he who humbles himself will be exalted" (Luke 18:9-14 NIV).

As long as we are busy flattering ourselves by affirming our own goodness and righteousness, we shut out the Spirit of revelation. This Spirit seeks to penetrate the veil in order to bring about a sober realization of our fallen condition. "For they, being ignorant of God's righteousness, and *seeking to establish their own righteousness*, have not submitted to the righteousness of God" (Romans 10:3). Submitting to the righteousness of God means recognizing that all have sinned and fallen short of the glory and righteousness of God. As it is written, "There is none righteous, no, not one" (Romans 3:10).

In the parable that we just read, the tax collector had come to a revelation that he had sinned against a holy God. Peter had this same revelation when he was confronted by the glory of God. "He fell down at Jesus' feet, saying, "Depart from me, for I am a sinful man, O Lord!" (Luke 5:8). This revelation of our sinful state before God is the primary evidence of the convicting work of the Holy Spirit who seeks to convict the world of sin, righteousness, and judgment (John 16:8). Jesus taught that unless we repent, we will all perish. But we will not repent unless the Holy Spirit convicts us of our need for repentance and reconciliation to a holy God.

As the Spirit of God broods over the vast company of unbelievers, He has been given the assignment to convict the world of sin and their lack of faith in God's Messiah. In fact, Jesus said, "He will convict the world of sin... because they do not believe in Me" (John 16:8, 9). We could rightly say that the unveiling of hearts appears to be the primary work of the Holy Spirit in the earth. In the Old Testament sin was revealed through the law. "For through the law comes the knowledge of sin" (Romans 3:20 NASB). But since the appearance of Christ, sin is now measured by people's response to the Saviour. The ultimate sin is the rejection of Christ.

Unveiling the Heart of the Believer

The initial revelation of the sinful and broken condition of the human heart is only the beginning. When the revelation of human sinfulness is met with heartfelt repentance and a cry for mercy, it results in salvation. Christ enters the human heart and we are supernaturally regenerated into new creations. But even after we are born again there is still an ongoing unveiling of the heart. The Spirit begins to reveal the heart of Christ in us, but there is still an unveiling of those places in our heart where we foolishly continue to walk according to the old selfish nature. The Holy Spirit continues to convict believers of sin in order to bring into the light those areas of darkness that the Lord seeks to purge from our hearts.

This is a strange paradox, but it is essential for believers to understand the ongoing need to receive an ever deepening unveiling of their old nature in order to promote deeper repentance. Fortunately, God doesn't reveal everything about the extent of our sin and brokenness all at once. I don't think we would be able to handle it. As we journey through life as a follower of Jesus, the Holy Spirit reveals the strongholds of darkness that hold us in bondage to sin. Repentance plays a vital role in the life of the believer. James said, "Confess your sins to each other and pray for each other so that you may be healed" (James 5:16 NIV). Our ongoing repentance paves the way for the realm of heaven to explode inside of us. Deep repentance ushers us into a joyous life of communion with God.

After conversion, the heart of a regenerated person is a curious mixture of the old and the new. We have Christ living at the centre of our heart—in our regenerated spirit—but we also have the legacy of the old sinful nature with all of its old thoughts, motives, and intentions. God has given us a brand new heart; this new heart is the very heart of Jesus imparted to our regenerated spirit. Like a hidden seed, God sows an entirely new nature into the core of our being. However, we still have to deal with everything that constitutes our old life. That life must be systematically stripped away and put to death through the power of the cross. In Christ we are dead to sin but we still must learn how to walk in the power of the cross.

Paul engaged in a delicate theological balancing act between these two realities. As the champion of new creation theology, nothing gave him greater joy than unveiling the miracle of the new birth and the reality that Christ now dwelt in the heart of every believer. However, Paul also spent considerable time pastoring the people of God. Time and again he had to expose those areas of believers' hearts where they were still walking according to the sinful nature, which created havoc in the church and in their relationships.

Paul continually called those under his pastoral care to a place of deeper repentance. Paul taught that the systematic unveiling of "the goodness of God leads you to repentance" (Romans 2:4). Paul rejoiced when the saints who were still ensnared in sin finally came to repentance and sorrow over their sins. "I see that my letter hurt you, but only for a little while – yet now I am happy, not because you were made sorry, but because your sorrow led you to repentance. For you became sorrowful as God intended" (2 Corinthians 7:8-9 NIV).

We see this same pattern in the post-resurrection ministry of Jesus to the churches. Whilst affirming the new creation, Jesus called New Testament believers to repentance whenever they chose to walk according to their old sinful nature. He said, "As many as I love, I rebuke and chasten. Therefore be zealous and repent" (Revelation

3:19). Repentance always opens the door to the fullness of the kingdom of heaven. Repentance is not a onetime response to God; it is intended to be a constant posture of our heart as we walk humbly with Him.

God reveals more and more of the subtleties of our old nature as we adjust to the intensity of the light. The Christian life is a continuum of deeper and deeper revelation, not only of the exceeding vile nature of sin, but also of the perfect and pure heart of Jesus Christ in us. God gives us a brand new heart but we still contend with the presence of indwelling sin. When the Lord said, "the heart is deceitful above all things and desperately wicked" (Jeremiah 17:9), He was describing the lost who did not know God. This is no longer an accurate description of the heart of born again believers. They are now saints who have been given a brand new nature in Christ. When a Christian sins, they betray their new identity, because they are living inconsistently with who they really are in Christ.

Every revelation of sin in the heart of the believer is always accompanied by a revelation of the cleansing power of the blood of Jesus and the unveiling of the heart of Christ in us. Whenever we see sin in our hearts, we immediately ought to ask: who is Jesus to me in this situation, and what aspect of His divine nature displaces the ugliness of my sin? The primary instrument that God uses to reveal the heart is the Word of God. As we have seen, the writer to the Hebrews tells us,

> The Word of God is living and powerful, and sharper than any two-edged sword, piercing even to the division of soul and spirit, and of joints and marrow, *and is a discerner of the thoughts and intents of the heart*" (Hebrews 4:12).

The sword of the Spirit separates soul from spirit for a very good reason. We are a "new man" in our spirit but our "old man" still seeks to rule and reign in the un-renewed regions of our soul. That "old man" must be exposed and, in Paul's words, "put off." He said, "Put off, concerning your former conduct, the old man which grows corrupt according to the deceitful lusts, and be renewed in the spirit of your mind, and… put on the new man which was created according to God, in true righteousness and holiness" (Ephesians 4:22-24).

Why is there a necessity for an ongoing unveiling of the old sinful nature if we are in fact new creations? The answer lies in our desperate need to discern the enemy of our own souls, and in this instance, I am not talking about the devil. Without a further unveiling of the "old man" we are flying blind and we do not know our own enemy. There is an old saying, "We have met the enemy and he is us!" We are indeed our own worst enemy and that is why God has to expose the unfruitful works of darkness in us. The *New International Version* of Hebrews 4:20 says that the Word of God "judges the thoughts and attitudes of the heart." This is clearly talking about the presence of the residual old nature that still lingers in the heart of believers. The *Amplified Version* says that the Word of God, "exposes, sifts and analyses the thoughts and purposes of the heart."

I personally love the *J.B. Phillips Translation* which says that the Word of God "cuts more keenly than any two-edged sword, it strikes through to the place where soul and spirit meet, to the innermost intimacies of a man's being; it examines the very thoughts and motives of a man's heart." The Word of God cuts to the very core of any remaining selfishness in the purposes, motives, and attitudes of the heart. These hidden heart realities still exercise power over our thought life, speech, behavior, and outward actions until they are systematically confronted and purged from our hearts through repentance.

Paul taught the necessity of "purging out the old leaven" (1 Corinthians 5:7). It is only as God begins to expose and deliver us from the old sinful and selfish orientation of our hearts that all of our outward behavior begins to change. That is why Jesus said, "First cleanse the inside of the cup, that the outside may be clean also" (Matthew 23:26). God always changes us from the inside out—this is the hidden work of the Spirit within our hearts.

We have seen that God confronts and exposes sin in the heart of the unbeliever in order to bring them to repentance and salvation, but He also confronts and exposes strongholds of sin in the life of the believer as well. God confronts sin universally, whether in the heart of the sinner or in the heart of the saint. Wherever sin appears, God commands us to repent. Remember the words of Jesus, "As many as I love, I rebuke and chasten. Therefore be zealous and repent" (Revelation 3:19).

It must have been just as hard for Jesus' earthly followers to recognise His rebukes as an expression of His love as it is for us today. But, seen from heaven's perspective, the exposure of human sinfulness is a pure gift from a loving God who desires our freedom more than we desire it ourselves. The bad news of human sinfulness always heralds the good news of God's free gift of salvation.

The Bible makes it clear that God intentionally wounds us with the revelation of our true condition before He can administer the remedy. "Come, let us return to the Lord. He has torn us to pieces but He will heal us; He has injured us but He will bind up our wounds. After two days He will revive us; on the third day He will restore us that we may live in His presence" (Hosea 6:1-2 NIV). No matter how painful, Jesus told people the truth but He always spoke the truth in love. "For whom the Lord loves He chastens" (Hebrews 12:6). Jesus practiced the proverb that said, "Open rebuke is better than love carefully concealed. Faithful are the wounds of a friend" (Proverbs 27:5-6).

These wounds are painful but extremely necessary. "Blows that hurt cleanse away evil, as do stripes the inner depths of the heart" (Proverbs 20:30). Paul acknowledged that his letter to the Corinthians had hurt them, but he was calling them to repentance. Isn't it true that the vast majority of people spend most of their lives avoiding the wounds of the truth? Mark Heard, one of my favorite Christian musicians from the 1980s, said, "The thoughts that I've avoided are the ones I need right now!"[4] Why do we so resist the truth when it has such incredible power to set us free? The addict never likes to face the reality of his addiction but this is the only thing that promises freedom.

The doctrine of the unknowability of the heart apart from divine revelation is the biblical starting point for all true Christian ministry. We cannot know our own heart without the Holy Spirit's ministry of divine revelation, and we cannot receive this ministry without deep heart repentance. There is a realm of the revelatory knowledge of the heart that only the repentant can enter. As hard as it sounds, the rest of the human race is left to languish in self-delusion and deception. Repentance is the key that unlocks the door to the knowledge of the heart.

The Bible is the most comprehensive road map of the human heart known to humanity. In fact, there is no other. It is unsurpassed in its depth of wisdom and its sheer relevance to the human predicament. God tells it like it is, and He tells it with amazing accuracy and insight. All who study the Scriptures are astonished to discover its incredible applicability to the human condition. God alone knows the human heart, yet He invites us into a place of revelation that has infinite power to set us free. This revelation also empowers us to set others free. Jesus said, "You shall know the truth, and the truth shall make you free" (John 8:32). There is a Friend who sticks closer than a brother and faithful are the wounds of this glorious Friend who courageously speaks the truth in love in order to set our hearts free.

Chapter Six

The Knowledge of the Heart of God

And this is eternal life, that they may know You, the only true God, and Jesus Christ whom You have sent.
(John 17:3)

June thought that she knew the Lord until the day she met Sarah. She had read the Bible for years and even led women's study groups, but deep within her heart she always felt there was something missing. She was part of a fellowship that was extremely cautious about the spiritual gifts, yet they were all eager to follow the Lord and to know Him. Sarah joined the fellowship because her husband had just moved to the city for a new job.

There was something about Sarah that all the women found greatly attractive. There was a depth to her spirituality and a grace that flowed from her lips whenever she spoke. When she ministered to the other women in the fellowship, it was as though the Lord opened the heavens. June's first encounter with Sarah was unforgettable. Sarah spoke into her life about the season she was in with the Lord and June began to weep as the Spirit touched her heart. Sarah was the mentor that June had always dreamed of and the Lord had heard her cry. Within six months, June's ministry in the church sprang to life and her heart was in a whole new place with the Lord.

Like June, we all meet those who know the Lord with a depth of intimacy that awakens a yearning in our hearts to know the Lord more intimately. Apollos, a brilliant young theologian from North Africa, had just such an encounter with a godly couple who were able to bring him into a much deeper knowledge of the ways of the Lord.

> A Jew named Apollos, an eloquent speaker who knew the Scriptures well, had just arrived in Ephesus from Alexandria in Egypt. He had been taught the way of the Lord and talked to others with great enthusiasm and accuracy about Jesus. However, he knew only about John's baptism. When Priscilla and Aquila heard him preaching boldly in the synagogue, they took him aside and explained the way of God more accurately (Acts 18:24-26 NLT).

The widespread lack of heart knowledge in the church can be directly attributed to the lack of personal revelation into the heart of God. Throughout its long history, much of the church has lacked this deep revelation of the heart of the Lord. We have known Him from a distance but few of us can claim to know Him intimately. Strange theologies have been invented and Christians have brutally persecuted their own brethren, all because people have not known the heart of their Heavenly Father. Jesus said, "They will do such things because they have not known the Father or me" (John 16:3 NIV). The Christian crusades to the Holy Land in the Middle Ages are a great example. These "Christian" crusaders shed the blood of thousands of Muslims in the name of Christ. The bloodshed in Northern Ireland between the Catholics and the Protestants reveals the same foolishness.

The revelation of the heart of God has a number of significant benefits for the believer. First, it gives us a prophetic benchmark by which we can assess the condition of our own hearts before Him. Second, it gives us a clear sense of vision of where the Lord is taking us in our own personal journey of the transformation of our heart.

Third, the revelation of the Father heart of God toward his children and the revelation of the ravished heart of the Heavenly Bridegroom toward His bride is intended to have a powerful transformational effect upon our own hearts.

Whenever we experience revelatory insight into the nature of God's heart it always has a profound and lasting impact on our own heart. The result is that it sheds increased light upon the depths of our emotional brokenness and any residual strongholds of sin in our hearts. This deeper, unfolding revelation is essential to promoting the kind of sincere heart repentance that the Scriptures call us to.

God is awesome in His holiness and He always seeks to sanctify the hearts of His people by calling them to repentance. "But as He who called you is holy, you also be holy in all your conduct, because it is written, 'Be holy, for I am holy'" (1 Peter 1:16). In the Old Testament, the Ten Commandments were a revelation of the holy requirements of a holy God. This self-disclosure of God's majestic perfection on Mount Sinai had profound implications for those who received it. God blasted the Israelites with a revelation of His holiness.

A number of years ago I was greatly impacted by a book by Mike Bickle called *Passion for Jesus*. In this powerful book Bickle discusses the spiritual impact that the revelation of the holiness of God has upon believers.

> When we begin to comprehend the excellencies of God's person, we will be horrified by the declining ethics and decaying morality in our churches and nation. Beholding the holiness and glory of God reveals the presence of sin and its terrible ugliness. A new revelation of God's holiness always shines the spotlight on our own condition.[5]

Knowing God from a distance inevitably results in a low view of the seriousness of sin and the depths of our brokenness before the Lord. The prophet Isaiah knew God, perhaps more intimately than any of his contemporaries, but when he had a face-to-face encounter with the Lord in His majestic holiness, he fell face down before Him and cried, "Woe is me, for I am undone! Because I am a man of unclean lips, and I dwell in the midst of a people of unclean lips; for my eyes have seen the King, The Lord of hosts" (Isaiah 6:5).

Whenever we grow in our knowledge of the heart of God it consistently takes us to a new level of revelation: into the true state of our own heart. For example, as an earthly father, I often contemplate the Father heart of God and it helps me to see how far short I fall in representing the heart of God to my own children. Whenever we gain fresh revelatory insight into the depths of the love of God, we realize how little we actually love as God loves us. The same is true of every new insight we receive into the heart of God, whether it is the mercy of God, the forgiveness of God, the kindness of God, or the faithfulness of God.

As we meditate upon the heart of Jesus Christ, we come face to face with the very heart of God because, as Paul taught, Jesus is the visible image of the invisible God (Colossians 1:15). Jesus said, "He who has seen Me has seen the Father" (John 14:9). Jesus' primary purpose was to reveal the heart of His Heavenly Father so that mankind could no longer say that they did not know what God was like. Everything He did, every look in His eyes, every gesture, and every word was an explicit revelation of the very heart of the Creator. The intense purity of the heart of Jesus highlights the uncleanness of the hearts of men.

The light that shone forth from His heart revealed how dark the human heart had become. The wholeness of the heart of Jesus revealed the depth of brokenness in the hearts of men. Jesus' capacity to relate to people exposed the relational dysfunction of his contemporaries. His integrity and his sincerity exposed the hypocrisy and pretence of those who walked in darkness. But in spite of the purity of every aspect of His life, many people were strangely drawn to Him because there was no sense of condemnation or superiority, only deep acceptance and a sense of genuine compassion and love.

Many Christians have only known Jesus as a distant figure from history. Even the idea that we can know Him personally and intimately is foreign to many in the church. Yet the concept of entering into an intimate, personal knowledge of the very heart of God lies at the centre of the Christian faith.

I consider myself greatly blessed because I was exposed to the ministry of A.W. Tozer in the early years of my Christian walk. One of my pastors handed me a book titled *The Knowledge of the Holy*, and in the preface to this wonderful little book, Tozer laments what he calls "the loss of the concept of majesty from the popular religious mind." He said,

> The church has surrendered her once lofty concept of God and has substituted for it one so low, so ignoble, as to be utterly unworthy of thinking, worshipping men. The low view of God entertained almost universally among Christians is the cause of a hundred lesser evils everywhere among us. Modern Christianity is simply not producing the kind of Christian who can appreciate or experience the life in the Spirit. The decline of the knowledge of the Holy has brought on our troubles. A rediscovery of the majesty of God will go a long way toward curing them. It is impossible to keep our moral practices sound or our inward attitudes right while our idea of God is erroneous or inadequate. The man who comes to a right belief about God is relieved of ten thousand temporal problems.[6]

Every Christian would do well to regularly review his or her concept of God. If we are honest, we can always have an upgrade on our concept of who God is and what He is like. The Holy Spirit is constantly at work in our lives to upgrade our revelation of the nature and character of God. Anyone who ever entertains thoughts about

God is in constant danger of falling into error through worshipping a "god" that is different from the true God revealed in Scripture.

We are equally in danger of anthropomorphism, which is the projection of human characteristics upon God. The Lord rebuked the children of Israel for falling into this error when He said, "You thought that I was altogether like you!" (Psalm 50:21). Again, let me quote Tozer, who demonstrated a profound insight into the constant danger of our descent into idolatry.

> Among the sins to which the human heart is prone, hardly any other is more hateful than idolatry, for idolatry is at bottom a libel on His character. The idolatrous heart assumes that God is other than He is and substitutes for the true God one made after its own likeness. Always this God will conform to the image of the one who created it. A "god" begotten in the shadow of a fallen heart will quite naturally be no true likeness of the true God. The essence of idolatry is the entertainment of thoughts about God that are unworthy of Him. The first step down for any church is taken when it surrenders its high opinion of God.[7]

But there is a further dimension to the unfolding revelation of God's heart. The unveiling of the nature of the heart of God is the cornerstone of personal transformation because it is the revelation of the specific likeness into which God is conforming His children. In Romans 8:29 we are told, "Those whom God foreknew he also predestined to be conformed to the likeness of his Son." Every time we receive a deeper revelation into God's heart we are gaining a greater vision of God's agenda for our own lives.

The life of Christ is constantly upheld in the New Testament as the benchmark of true Christian spirituality. We are called to love as Christ loves (John 13:34), to forgive as Christ forgives (Ephesians 4:32), to walk as Christ walks (1 John 2:6), and to think as Christ thinks (1 Corinthians 2:16). Jesus raised the standard even higher when He said, "You are to be perfect, even as your Father in heaven is perfect" (Matthew 5:48).

Subsequently there is a strong element of spiritual warfare surrounding the unveiling of the heart of God. Satan understands the power released in the human heart when a person catches even a small glimpse, through the revelation of the Holy Spirit, of the magnificent heart of our glorious Creator. Paul taught that the *cornerstone* of our personal transformation into the image of God is the unveiling of the glorious heart of God.

> And all of us, with unveiled faces, seeing the glory of the Lord as though reflected in a mirror, are being transformed into the same image from one degree of glory to another; for this comes from the Lord, the Spirit (2 Corinthians 3:18 NRSV).

If Satan can hinder our reception to this life-changing revelation of the glory of God, then he knows that we can never be truly transformed in our hearts. He will do everything in his power to reinforce false concepts of God in our thought life and to blind our hearts to the true knowledge of God. But it is the work of the Holy Spirit to bring us to this glorious unveiling of the heart of God. "For it is the God who commanded light to shine out of darkness, who has shone in our hearts to give the light of the knowledge of the glory of God in the face of Jesus Christ" (2 Corinthians 4:6). Again, Mike Bickle writes:

> The great need of the church is to see, know and discover the indescribable glory of who God is. Seeing the heart, mind and character of God will cure our compromise and instability and motivate us to righteousness and holy passion. Personal, experiential knowledge of the person of Jesus will fuel obedience and zeal. It will put a stop to our restlessness and discontent. A new depth of intimacy will extinguish our

boredom and capture our hearts. The enemy has assaulted the people of God. He has weakened and destroyed our foundation of the knowledge of God. But in His arsenal God has reserved the secret weapon of all the ages – the awesome knowledge of the splendor of the person of Jesus.[8]

If we are to grow in the prophetic knowledge of the heart, we must understand that the unfolding revelation of the heart of God is the cornerstone of personal transformation. There are dimensions of revelation into the nature of God that are like keys that unlock the heart. Without this specific kind of revelation the human heart can never be changed in the way that God intends.

That is why Paul wrote, "I keep asking that the God of our Lord Jesus Christ, the glorious Father, may give you the Spirit of wisdom and revelation, *so that you may know him better*" (Ephesians 1:17 NIV). Heart revelation is the key. The central thesis of Mike Bickle's book, *Passion For Jesus,* is that we only grow in passion for the Son of God as His heart is supernaturally revealed to us by revelation. I would strongly encourage everyone to read this life-transforming book.

> The Holy Spirit unveils to us the passions and pleasures in the personality of the Son of God. This new insight into the heart of Jesus captures our hearts in a fresh way, and our spirits are energized and opened to new depths of passion for Him. There must come a time in the lives of mature believers when we are awakened to holy fervency. The progression of passion starts with this fresh awakening to holy fervency. It takes God to love God. It takes a progressive revelation of God's infinitely satisfying love, His exuberant affections and His indescribable beauty to awaken the church and to compel her to give herself wholly back to Him.[9]

These realities of "holy passion" and "being awakened to spiritual fervency" are so foreign to so many of us. Yet as we contemplate the fiery passion and fervency of the heart of Jesus, we cannot escape the conclusion that we are being transformed into the very image of Christ. We are also called by God to reflect this intense passion and fervency in our love for God, Himself. We cannot muster up this kind of intense spiritual passion. It is imparted to the heart that is awakened by His fiery passion.

As we draw near to the consuming fire of His holy presence, our hearts spontaneously combust and we are set on fire for God. If we maintain this intimacy with God, the fire of His presence will remain upon us, just as fire visibly descended on the heads of the disciples on the Day of Pentecost. Jesus has come to baptize His people in the Holy Spirit and fire. His love is like a fire that transforms us into "burning ones."

The revelatory knowledge of the heart of God is absolutely indispensable to the transformation of the human heart. All that we see of the heart of God, revealed in the person of Christ, becomes the promise of our own transformation into the image and likeness of Christ. The unveiling of the heart of Christ *to us* is the precursor to the unveiling of the heart of Christ *in us*.

The Israelites spied out the Promised Land long before they took possession of the land, yet they never let go of the promise of possessing the land. Whatever we see by revelation, we can possess by faith. God unveils His heart to us because He has promised to unveil His heart in us. That is the process of the transformation of the heart. Whatever we can see by revelation, we can have!

Jesus took the revelation of the heart of God to a whole new level. He revealed God as our loving Heavenly Father whose heart is bursting with tender affection toward all of humanity. The Old Testament revealed the holiness of God and His love for righteousness and justice, but the New Testament revelation of God was a massive upgrade.

There are so few references to God as our Father in the Old Testament that we can count them on one hand. Jesus was more than a prophet – He was the Son of God. And as the one and only Son of the Father, He was uniquely placed to unveil the heart of the Father. It takes a Son to reveal the Father! Jesus redefined prophetic ministry. The heart of His prophetic revelation to humanity was the unveiling of His wonderful Father in Heaven.

All those who have received Christ have been adopted into the family of God. Jesus introduces us to His Father, and this is the greatest prophetic act of all history. The revelation of the Father heart of God is the ultimate expression of prophetic ministry. It is the benchmark by which all subsequent prophetic ministry must be measured. Drawing us into intimate relationship with God as our Father is a stroke of prophetic genius.

Now that we have a Father in Heaven, everything must change around that single reality. Our lives are now gloriously trapped in the orbit of a loving Father who is intent on drawing us into the full expression of divine sonship. Nothing will ever be the same once the unconditional love of our Father begins to transform every area of our lives into the image of His Son through the prophetic unveiling of the heart of the Father. This is the knowledge of the heart of God that begins to change everything on the inside. Our entire approach to God is revolutionized when we sit before Him and meditate upon the intentionality of His heart toward us. We will no longer feel as though we are trying to initiate relationship with a holy and distant God. Instead, as our vision of the intentionality of God increases, we are drawn into a consciousness that we are being lovingly pursued. When I close my eyes in prayer, He is already there studying me with love and yearning for my fellowship. There is nothing like the revelation of the intentionality of the heart of God to deliver us from our religious striving, which constantly makes us feel as though we have to do all the initiating!

Chapter Seven

The Intimacy Paradigm

> The amazing grace of the Master, Jesus Christ, the extravagant love of God [the Father] and the *intimate friendship* of the Holy Spirit be with all of you.
> (2 Corinthians 13:14 The Message)

Jeremy had attended church for over twenty years. He knew the Bible well and made it his goal to read through the entire Old and New Testament at least once a year. He had studied theology at one of the best theological colleges in England and had been awarded two degrees in biblical studies and historical theology. He even lectured on theology in his own church. His son attended a charismatic church and had been inviting him to attend a service there for the past four years. Out of politeness he decided that he would finally acquiesce to his son's invitation.

As he sat in church that morning, the preacher spoke about the call to intimacy with God and Jeremy realized just how far he felt from God. In fact, more often than not, he felt distant from God and his heart felt cold and indifferent toward the Lord. As he reflected on the sermon, he realized that the whole subject of intimacy with God was little more than a vague concept. It was not something that had ever really been on his theological radar. The subject made him feel uncomfortable and his mind drifted off the words of the preacher to the safety of the familiar. His visit to a charismatic church that day was not an experience he was quick to want to repeat.

The first decade of my own spiritual journey was similarly characterized by the avoidance of intimacy. There were much easier subjects to master – subjects that I found manageable, and did not threaten my sense of control. I filled my life with theological teaching that rarely touched on the subject of intimacy, and I was largely content to avoid the subject altogether.

In 1990, I attended a Vineyard conference where the theme of intimacy with God was centre stage. My whole framework was profoundly challenged and my life was turned upside down. I was confronted with a quality and depth of ministry that was foreign to me. The speakers were flowing in the prophetic, and words of knowledge were freely flowing through their lives. They were ministering into areas of the heart that hindered authentic intimacy with God and offering healing prayer to hundreds of broken lives. People streamed forward at the invitation and many people went through dramatic deliverance.

My life was transformed by that single conference. I had undergone a profound paradigm shift. I had embraced what I now call the *intimacy paradigm*. I had turned a corner, theologically and conceptually. This set in motion a journey of moving from the head to the heart in order to become established in this new paradigm. Living exclusively from my head was no longer an option. I had been upgraded to a new level of reality and I could never be the same again. Living in the intimacy paradigm of an authentic heart journey with God has been the greatest challenge of my life as a believer. The Vineyard movement in the 1980s and 1990s were renowned for their pioneer work in new frontiers of intimate worship. Their CD series, *Touching the Father's Heart*, helped me to go much deeper in my heart journey of devotion.

The Intimacy Paradigm

The centerpiece in this battle to lay hold of the revelatory knowledge of the heart of God, is the pursuit of intimacy with God. If we are content to merely know God from a distance—to know *about* Him instead of knowing Him personally, experientially, and intimately—then that is all we will ever attain. I once heard a preacher facetiously say, "Blessed are those who expect nothing; they shall not be disappointed!" God has called us to such a depth of intimacy in relationship with Him that it massively transcends our intellectual comprehension. "Eye has not seen, nor ear heard, nor have entered into the heart of man the things which God has prepared for those who love Him" (1 Corinthians 2:9).

Paul taught that this intimate knowledge of the heart of God completely transcends our intellectual faculties. Theological knowledge is merely an invitation into the deep waters of spiritual intimacy. Those who have come into relationship with God through the new birth are now privileged "to know the love of Christ that surpasses knowledge" (Ephesians 3:19). This includes all theological knowledge.

And of course, God in His brilliance has already made a way for us. Through the new birth, He places us in Christ, planting us right in the fiery centre of that most intimate of all relationships: the relationship between the Father and His Beloved Son. This new intimacy is a gift. It is not something we earn! John said, "Everyone who confesses that Jesus is God's Son participates continuously in an intimate relationship with God" (1 John 4:15 The Message).

Intimacy with God is intended to be the defining characteristic of the Christian. Oneness that is characterized by deep supernatural love is the essence of true spiritual intimacy. Every Christian is intended to carry the aroma of divine intimacy so that their very presence invites others into their own experience of intimacy with God. Paul said, "Pray for the insight and ability to bring others into that intimacy" (1 Corinthians 14:13 The Message).

We read in the Psalms a brief phrase that powerfully captures this call to radical intimacy with God: "Deep calls unto deep" (Psalm 42:7). The inner depths of God's heart cries out for intimate fellowship with the deepest places in the hearts of His children. We were designed and fashioned for intimate relationship, not only with God but also with other human beings. God is the very author of intimacy and He has created us in such a way that we will never be satisfied unless we experience this gift of deep spiritual intimacy. Gordon and Gail MacDonald, in the opening paragraph of their book, *Heart Connections*, discuss the nature of this intimacy.

> If food is fuel for the stomach, intimacy is fuel for the soul. Without the one there is physical starvation, without the other there can be spiritual starvation. Intimacy implies a deep and lasting connection between persons. Age, intellect, class, gender, and all other such classifications are all irrelevant when it comes to experiencing this intense rapport. Yet some of the most intelligent and powerful people in our lives appear to know almost nothing about intimacy.[10]

As appealing as the concept may be, it has proven as elusive to humanity as the proverbial pot of gold at the end of the rainbow. For try as we will to reach this place where two hearts meet and stay connected, the promise somehow continues to elude us. As a pastor, the number one complaint I hear from people is the sense of not being able to connect with God in their hearts. The Apostle John came to the conclusion that the same factors that destroy intimacy with one another were the very same things that hinder intimacy with God. "If someone says, 'I love God,' and hates his brother, he is a liar; for he who does not love his brother whom he has seen, how can he love God whom he has not seen" (1 John 4:20)?

Intimacy is all about relationships, whether that relationship is with God, our spouse, children, parents, or friends. Whenever we come face to face with a roadblock in growing closer to another person, we will inevitably find that this very same issue will hinder us in drawing nearer to God. Our human relationships become a mirror that reflects the depth (or lack of depth) of our intimacy with God. Intimacy has to look like something! John said, "Anyone who claims to be intimate with God ought to live the same kind of life Jesus lived" (1 John 2:6 The Message).

The moment we purpose in our hearts to cultivate intimacy with God, we *must* begin to deal with the deeper issues of the heart. Intimacy is all about the connection of two hearts. Just as a married couple must work at cultivating intimacy in their marriage, so we must work at developing a closer walk with God. But if a Christian never sets their heart to pursue intimacy with God, they will never come to understand just how many roadblocks there are in our hearts to growing in intimacy.

The tragedy is that many Christians are content to know all about God without ever experiencing the gentle touch of His warm embrace. This comes when we seek to gain a firsthand, experiential knowledge of His heart. But once we embark upon this journey, there is no going back. This is the "intimacy paradigm" and it is an essential ingredient in developing a biblical understanding of the heart. For far too many Christians this intimate relational paradigm is totally foreign. We are strangers to the experiential knowledge of God, and we have somehow become acclimatized to this sub-standard level of Christian experience.

Many Christians are satisfied merely knowing about God and knowing intellectually that He cares about us and that our sins are forgiven. This, after all, is a considerable improvement upon our former condition when we were completely ignorant of God. But this stops way short of all that God has for us. It is very often a case of the good getting in the way of the best. This adage tends to summarize the lives of the vast majority of Christians. We settle for things that are good but we neglect those things that are best.

God's agenda in the redemption of our souls is to restore to us all that was lost in the Garden of Eden, where Adam walked with God in a deep spiritual union. Gordon MacDonald draws out the implications that the fall exercised upon our capacity to experience intimacy.

> The Book of Genesis describes a magnificent garden where the first man and woman made their home. Their ability to communicate and experience companionship seems to have been unlimited. But what is clear is that the first man and woman made an unfortunate series of choices. Intimacy – the close connection of people – was dealt a crippling blow. It was as if everything that had been created to be in harmony suddenly fell into conflict and dissonance. The first loss of intimacy resulted in estrangement from God. God came searching for them and found them hiding, ashamed of their choices, strangely embarrassed over their now-naked appearance. For the first time they had something unfortunate to hide, a secret they wanted to keep from their Maker, and that seriously diminished their relationship with Him. Ever since that day, humankind has tended to hide from God, but still He comes in search of us. God is forever seizing the initiative to establish intimacy with those who choose to stop hiding.
>
> Because of disobedience, the possibility of intimacy between Adam and Eve was also shattered. They began to blame each other when the heat was turned on. Adam displayed for all humanity the proud heart that blames others for the consequences of deeds and attitudes, even if it effectively destroys connection between people. Adam and Eve's once intensely intimate relationship simply ceased to exist. Today we struggle in our pursuit of intimacy because of those shattered relationships. That old, old story from the garden explains why we feel such a strong urge for intimacy and why it so often eludes us.[11]

The Intimacy Paradigm

Apart from Eugene Petersen's *Message Bible*, (which is really a paraphrase version) nowhere in Scripture do we find the word intimacy. But the concept of intimacy is embedded deep within the biblical idea of fellowship and love. Through this lens we understand that the Bible breathes the concept of intimacy from cover to cover. Agape love is commonly defined as a selfless choice to pursue the highest good of another person.

Agape love is much greater than this common definition would let on. There is a dimension of warmth, care, and sensitivity to others in the biblical concept of love that brings us into a *deep heart connection* with other people. Jesus calls us to love one another in such a way that we re-connect with each other on a profoundly intimate level. True love always draws our hearts into a sense of emotional engagement. This capacity to truly connect with others and with God is intended to be the defining characteristic of Jesus' disciples. Jesus said, "A new commandment I give to you, that you love one another; as I have loved you, that you also love one another. By this all will know that you are My disciples, if you have love for one another" (John 13:34-35).

This restoration of intimate, loving fellowship between human beings is unquestionably one of the most radical concepts in the Bible. Paul said, "The goal of this command is *love*, which comes from a pure heart and a good conscience and a sincere faith" (1 Timothy 1:5 NIV). The biblical evidence of Christian maturity is genuine love that flows from a heart that has been purified from sin and self-centeredness. "Now that you have purified yourselves by obeying the truth so that you have sincere love for your brothers, love one another deeply, from the heart" (1 Peter 1:22 NIV).

Biblical love is the very antithesis of sin and selfishness. In fact, sin is defined as the *transgression of the law* (see 1 John 3:4 KJV), whereas love is defined as the *fulfilment of the law* (see Romans 13:10). The whole reason God purifies our hearts from sin is to release us to truly love one another. A heart that entertains sin is incapacitated when it comes to love. As long as selfishness reigns in the human heart people disqualify themselves from being capable of loving. God can continually pour His love in but it will never flow out of a selfish soul.

Sincere love from the heart is a radical and challenging concept. It clearly implies the restoration of intimacy in relationships. Larry Crabb, in his book *Understanding People*, suggests that we have *redefined* Christian maturity in order to side step the radicalism of the call to authentic Christian love. He contrasts two starkly different models of Christian maturity.

> Maturity is often defined in terms of knowledge, habits and skills. People who know the Scriptures, who do what they should, and don't do what they shouldn't, and who can effectively serve in Christian activities may be regarded as mature. But often those who have the trappings of maturity don't seem to draw us to the Lord. We may be impressed, challenged and stimulated – but not *drawn*. Truly mature people… entice us to pursue a God whom they know better than we.

What then is maturity? Maturity will be most clearly visible in the way people relate to one another. Bible study habits, church activities, frequency of witnessing, discipline in lifestyle, time spent in prayer, willingness to sacrifice personal comforts, spending patterns – each of these is important but all can be evident without maturity as their basis. The core of maturity is fundamentally visible in our relational patterns. A mature pattern of relating involves whatever actions represent the abandonment of self-protection. In a word, the visible evidence of maturity is love.

The more I reflect on the love that Paul spoke of in 1 Corinthians 13, the more I am persuaded that few people love. People who love, I suggest, are not always those who look the most loving. Nice people are not hard to find. Churches, neighborhood parties, and civic clubs are full of friendly people. Gracious people who would never make you the object of unkind jest are known to all of us. But *loving* people are in short supply. Compliments, warm smiles and affectionate pats never define love. So much of what passes for Christian community represents the well-developed art of graciously distancing one another for purposes of personal comfort. To love means to come toward another person without self-protection, to esteem others greater than ourselves. Our Lord, as always, is the supreme example.[12]

The bottom line is that we are all motivated, in varying degrees, by a *fear of intimacy*. We fear this because ever since the Garden of Eden we have had to protect ourselves from the pain that inevitably comes through human relationships. Sin has brought division, disharmony, shame, and rejection into every human relationship and the experience of rejection is sometimes just too hard to bear.

It is far easier to avoid intimacy in relationships, especially as we begin to learn that rejection and the dreaded inevitability of relational breakdown is part of the package. Our quest to avoid the pain that comes in relationships causes us to value the protection of our own hearts above the value of pursuing intimacy with others. As long as self-protection is our primary goal, we will never learn to love as Jesus loves.

If we would grow in our knowledge of the heart, we must first understand that the *doorway* to a deep transformation of the heart is the pursuit of intimacy. To the believers in Philippi, Paul wrote, "And this is my prayer: that your love may abound more and more in knowledge and depth of insight" (Philippians 1:9 NIV). If love is the evidence of Christian maturity and if the capacity to cultivate intimacy in relationships is the essence of love, then we must pursue intimacy with all of our being. Only then will we grow in the kind of love that Jesus and Paul described.

Because God tenaciously pursues the restoration of intimacy with His children, He is faithful to reveal to us everything in our lives that hinders our growth in intimacy. Subsequently, every aspect of our human relationships becomes a school of the heart as God trains us in the art of cultivating intimacy. All of life becomes a classroom, and every experience becomes a lesson as we press toward the goal of love that flows from a pure heart.

In order to embrace the intimacy paradigm, we must learn to cultivate the intuitive dimension of the heart. We may very well have a cognitive understanding of the concepts of intimacy and love, but the realities of these concepts are embodied in the *experience* of love. The art of Christian love and intimacy is better caught than taught. There is always a valid place for intellectual analysis in the Christian life, but the experience of intimacy transcends rational analysis. It is an experience! As I mentioned in the first chapter, my own personal journey has been one of a slow and gradual deliverance from an unfeeling heart. My capacity to feel and to express my feelings has been deeply compromised because I came from a highly unfeeling family. This was not their fault; they were also the product of unfeeling parents where emotions were something to be avoided. Many people have grown up in a family where feelings were never expressed, and this can exercise a crippling effect upon the heart. It creates a deep wound because love was never expressed, and love simply cannot grow in an unfeeling heart.

Our heart is that part of us which is able to experience the intimate touch of our loving Heavenly Father, whereas our minds are capable only of intellectual analysis. If God seeks to draw us into intimacy with Himself, He will not appeal to the intellect but to the heart. In fact, intellectual analysis has the capacity to kill all intimacy! Many Christians are so locked into analysis mode that they are unable to experience any kind of intimacy with God. I often feel as though my own spiritual journey has largely been characterized by an attempt to escape the vice-like grip of cold heartedness where so often I find myself continually stuck in my head. And I know that many other Christians can testify to the same struggle.

The Paralysis of Analysis

If our rational and intellectual faculties stand in the way of entering into an intimate relationship with the Lord, then analysis must be recognized as a stronghold of the mind that is capable of hindering our spiritual growth. It is an undeniable fact that there is a romantic dimension to the biblical definition of our relationship with the Lord. Many good books have been written on the topic of the divine romance that characterizes the relationship between Christ and His bride. But romance and intimacy can only be experienced in the heart.

The Song of Solomon, which has historically been understood by the church to allegorically depict the love relationship between Christ and His bride, opens with these words, "Let him kiss me with the kisses of his mouth; for your love is better than wine" (Song of Songs 1:2). When the Bridegroom metaphorically kisses us in our hearts, we *experience* His tender and intimate affection toward us. We are exhorted in the Psalms to "Kiss the Son" (Psalm 2:12). This is our prescribed love response to the kisses of His mouth.

It is interesting that in Greek the word *worship* actually means to kiss. The word worship is the English translation of the Greek word *proskuneo,* which is derived from two Greek words: *pros* meaning toward and *kuneo* meaning to kiss. When we worship the Lord, we are actually kissing Him.

Analysis has no place in romance. If someone were to analyze the concept of kissing, they would probably never do it. Couples kiss because it is a wonderful experience; it stirs and awakens the emotions. As an expression of romantic intimacy, kissing is exclusively a matter of the heart.[13] There is a deep mystical dimension to our relationship with the Heavenly Bridegroom that those who are ensnared by a cold, cerebral rationalism find offensive to the mind. But this is the substance of the heart of the worshipper.

Some believers are intellectually on fire but their hearts are emotionally cold. Even back in the 1950s, Tozer said that "the dividing line today is between evangelical rationalists and evangelical mystics."[14] That is, between those who are content with an intellectual faith that is centred in the mind and those who hunger to enter into an intimate union with the Father in their hearts. John Wimber, the father of the Vineyard Movement, succinctly illustrates this distinction between the heart and the mind in his book, *The Dynamics of Spiritual Growth*.

> Over the years I have observed that Christians tend to fall into two camps: subjectivists and rationalists. Subjectivists emphasise experience, sometimes at the expense of knowledge of the Bible. Rationalists, in a never-ending search for "objective truth," are suspicious of spiritual experience. Their fear of experience can leave them spiritually dry. Both extremes are wrong. Both divide experience and truth, which are meant to go together. Subjectivists can fall into the trap of seeking experience for its own sake. Rationalists can become tied to a corpse of dead orthodoxy, studying the Bible yet somehow avoiding knowing the God who wrote it. God's revelation must penetrate our hearts in order to change how we live. The analogy of a match and oxygen captures the dynamic relationship between the two. A match will remain lit only if sufficient oxygen is present to feed its flame. If oxygen is in short supply, the flame will have no staying power. Information about God is like the match; spiritual experience is like the oxygen. We need both.[15]

No one with a basic knowledge of contemporary church history and an awareness of the present strengths and weaknesses of the evangelical church would dispute the fact that the centre of gravity in evangelicalism is clearly tilted toward a rationalistic expression of the Christian faith rather than a subjective expression. The answer, of course, is not to shift the centre of gravity so far toward subjectivism that we create further imbalance. Rather, we need to find the biblical balance between the intuitive and the cognitive.

We are called to intimacy with God in the context of a rational understanding of the truth of the Scriptures. Indeed, this is the balanced position because the experience of intimacy with God is the very focal point of the Scriptures. Jesus said, "This is eternal life, that they may *know You*, the only true God, and Jesus Christ whom You have sent" (John 17:3). But when we say that our experience of intimacy with God has to be set in the context of rationality, we need to guard against the danger of limiting ourselves from some of the deep mystical encounters experienced by the great mystics of church history. These mystics experienced the love of God in such raptures of mystical delight that they were rendered drunk, intoxicated by the wine of Christ's mystical love.

Fortunately, there are many accounts of wild, ecstatic encounters with the wine of love throughout the Scriptures. We can be assured that no matter how intense the raptures of mystical bliss that we may experience in our lives, there has always been someone in the Bible who already experienced these peak mystical experiences of the love of God. The intimate love of Christ, the Heavenly Bridegroom, can become so intense that *intoxication* is the closest word to describe the intensity of such mystical and rapturous ecstasies. I began having these kinds of mystical encounters in the mid 1990s, and they have been the best things that have ever happened to me as a Christian.

Knowing God intimately and knowing His heart toward us is the very essence of the Christian life. Intimacy with God is the foundation of every aspect of the Christian life. Without this intimate knowledge of God's heart, we cannot enter into the fullness of our calling to participate with Christ in revealing the Father. This is the ultimate purpose of the intimacy paradigm, and God is actively seeking to promote this paradigm shift among His people. Paul asserted that it is our high calling in God to pursue this intimate knowledge of the heart of God.

> I count all things to be loss in view of the surpassing value of *knowing* Christ Jesus my Lord, for whom I have suffered the loss of all things, and count them but rubbish so that I may gain Christ, and may be found in Him... *that I may know Him* and the power of His resurrection... Not that I have already obtained all this, or have already been made perfect, but I press on to take hold of that for which Christ Jesus took hold of me. Brothers, I do not consider myself yet to have taken hold of it. But one thing I do: Forgetting what is behind and straining toward what is ahead, I press on toward the goal to win the prize for which God has called me heavenward in Christ Jesus (Philippians 3:8-14 NIV).

Intimacy and the Prophetic

The release of the prophetic is predicated on the development of intimacy in the life of the believer. Prophetic insight and wisdom flows spontaneously out of the cultivation of intimacy with God. Heart prophets are the champions of intimacy. They understand that without intimacy there cannot be anything of the prophetic manifest through their lives. Their call to the church is to embrace the intimacy paradigm and for the saints to invest their lives into the cultivation of intimacy with the Lord.

Prophets minister out of the wealth of their prophetic knowledge of the heart of God. They minister effectively into the hearts of those who heed their call to move forward into intimacy. But for those who reject the call to cultivate intimacy, there is little that they have to offer. All they can hope to achieve is to keep knocking on the door and beckoning the saints to hear the voice of the Good Shepherd as He urges His people to embrace the call to intimacy. The ministry of the prophet must always resemble the ministry of Jesus.

A number of years back, a brother told me that he couldn't see why we needed the gift of prophecy in the church. His understanding of the prophetic was a little bit different to my own. He thought that prophetic ministry was simply proclaiming the truths of the Bible in the power of the Holy Spirit. He pointed to the text that said, "Do not despise prophetic utterances. But examine everything carefully; hold fast to that which is good" (1 Thessalonians 5:20,21). He reasoned that if everything a prophet said needed to be tested by the Scriptures then why do we need prophets if all the saints now have access to the Scriptures? His argument sounded logical but only if *his* particular understanding of the nature of prophetic ministry was biblical.

I explained to him my own understanding of the nature of prophetic ministry. I suggested that prophecy was a declaration of the heart and mind of God for a specific person or group of people in a specific season or situation in their life. Prophecy is a *"word in season"* for those who are weary (Isaiah 50:4). There is always a forth-telling in the prophetic, but it can sometimes cross over into foretelling the future because the Holy Spirit sometimes shows us "things to come" (John 16:13). The bread and butter of prophetic ministry is forth-telling but it is occasionally enhanced by foretelling.

Prophecy is the communication of God's heart and mind to a particular person in order to convey that God knows them intimately and understands their struggles yet still loves them in spite of all that He sees in their heart. Paul taught that prophecy makes known the secrets of the heart. "If all prophesy, and an unbeliever or an uninformed person comes in, he is convinced by all, he is convicted by all. And thus the *secrets of his heart* are revealed; and so, falling down on his face, he will worship God and report that God is truly among you" (1 Corinthians 14:24-26).

Rather than the Scriptures rendering prophetic ministry redundant, the Scriptures themselves invite us into a realm of deep prophetic insight. Through Scripture we see into the heart of God and we gain a prophetic insight into the heart of the person who is in need of a prophetic encounter. The operation of the Spirit of prophecy is therefore predicated upon a certain level of intimacy with God. Those who are beginning to flow in this dimension of Jesus' kingdom ministry eagerly invite their brethren into a life of intimacy with our Heavenly Father.

This is the life that Jesus modelled to His disciples and the lifestyle to which He called them. They embraced the challenge and purposed in their hearts to pursue intimacy with God. As they adopted the lifestyle of prayer, they eventually discovered that they were equipped to flow in the prophetic just as Jesus was when He was still among them. Intimacy is all about drawing near to the heart of the Father and listening to His voice. Then we simply report what we hear the Lord saying.

Growth in intimacy, both with God and with one another, is the very essence of true spirituality. This is the true heart journey that God calls us to embark upon. The intimacy paradigm will turn your world upside down and it will turn your heart inside out. Don't worry, it is meant to! This is the standard to which every Christian is called. Anything less is shallow religion!

As we examine our own personal heritage in the church, we need to consider the kinds of influence that have been exercised by pastors and teachers over our lives. For those of us who have spent decades in the church, we have a spiritual family of origin. For some believers, their spiritual family of origin has been deeply dysfunctional. Some Christians have grown up in an exclusively rationalist expression of the faith and they have literally been messed up by spiritual leaders who have imparted their own fear of intimacy into the sheep. The spirit behind this kind of ministry is often a spirit of unbelief.

Others may have grown up in charismatic or Pentecostal traditions that have emphasized prophecy and the power of the Holy Spirit. Yet even in these kinds of churches there is no guarantee that there has been a deep call to intimacy, instruction in how to cultivate intimacy with God, and guidance toward an authentic heart journey. Each of us needs to be aware of the spiritual influences that have been exercised in our lives. Sometimes the pursuit of an intimate heart journey can be negatively shaped by our personal history. We need to take our cues from the Good Shepherd who is committed to converting us to the fullness of the heart revolution. Jesus lives within the intimacy paradigm and He is seeking to establish us in this foundational kingdom core value.

Chapter Eight

The Wise and Foolish Virgins

> Five of them were foolish and five were wise. The foolish ones took their lamps but did not take any oil with them. The wise, however, took oil in jars along with their lamps.
> (Matthew 25:2-4 NIV)

Colin was a theology student at one of the leading theological colleges in his city. He had been studying full time for the ministry for over three years and had been achieving excellent grades. His professors were encouraging him to consider pursuing a Masters degree in theology and to seriously think about becoming a lecturer in historical and systematic theology. He had some good friends from his old youth group who had become involved in a charismatic church that was renowned for its wonderful worship. Colin reluctantly responded to the invitation to come but he was automatically suspicious of charismatic Christians because he found them far too emotional.

His fears were realized when he found himself in an immersive worship gathering that went far too long for his liking. As he looked around the room he saw hundreds of young people his age swept up in intimate worship, some with tears falling down their faces. He didn't get it and he couldn't wait for it to be over. He despised what he called "excessive emotionalism" and told his friends that it was definitely not for him. Colin retreated to the safety of his evangelical Bible study group where they would always sing at least a couple of unemotional worship song before the study commenced.

Jesus calls us to a life of intimate prayer and worship in the Secret Place. He anticipated that His faithful and true disciples would adopt His lifestyle of withdrawing from the flurry of human existence into a place of regular intimate encounter with God. Jesus modeled this lifestyle to His disciples and they recognized that it was the key to His ability to maintain a life of spiritual refreshment. "Now it came to pass in those days that He went out to the mountain to pray and continued all night in prayer to God" (Luke 6:12).

"One day Jesus was praying in a certain place. When He finished, one of his disciples said to Him, 'Lord, teach us to pray'" (Luke 11:1 NIV). Jesus gave specific instructions to His disciples in both how to pray and what to pray. In response to this request in the Gospel of Luke, Jesus taught His disciples to pray what has been called the Lord's Prayer, but it really ought to be described as the disciple's prayer. Jesus also instructed His disciples *how* to pray as He prayed by withdrawing from the world to a place of solitude where the disciple draws near to God in the Secret Place.

"But you, when you pray, go into your inner room, close your door and pray to your Father who is in the Secret Place, and your Father who sees what is done in secret will reward you openly" (Matthew 6:6 NASB). Jesus taught that the person who invests him or herself into an authentic heart to heart relationship with God is truly wise. "Therefore whoever hears these sayings of Mine, and does them, I will liken him to a wise man who built his house on the rock: and the rain descended, the floods came, and the winds blew and beat on that house; and it did not fall, for it was founded on the rock. But everyone who hears these sayings of Mine, and does not do them, will be like a foolish man who built his house on the sand: and the rain descended, the floods came, and the winds blew and beat on that house; and it fell. And great was its fall" (Matthew 7:24-27). This final section of the Sermon on the Mount has specific relevance to the call to a life of obedient prayer that is done in secret.

In his *Lectures on Revival,* Charles Finney wrote a challenging article titled, "The Backslider in Heart." His key text was Proverbs 14:14, "The backslider in heart will be filled with his own ways, but a good man will be satisfied from above." In this sermon Finney points out that the key indicator of a backslidden heart is the neglect of the Secret Place.

> The backslider is any one who was once converted, but who does not enjoy secret prayer, and hold daily communion with God. A man may keep up the form of prayer, he may be on his knees a great deal, and yet have no communion with God – not feel that God is present with him. He may pray ever so much, in form, and yet have no spirit of prayer. If in your secret prayer you do not actually draw near to God, you are either a backslider in heart or a hypocrite. No matter to what church you belong, or what office you hold, or what character you may bear in the sight of men; God regards you as a backslider, if you do not enjoy the spirit of prayer. A person may be known as a backslider, when his secret prayers are short, and far between. Persons who enjoy prayer, pray very frequently. If you pray but seldom, or if you do not pray as often as you eat, or do not spend much time in communion with God as you do in gratifying your appetite, it is a sign you have backslidden. You did not do so when you enjoyed your first love. Then you had rather pray than eat. Your feeling was, that if you must cut short one, you would say; let the body fast, but my soul must be fed. It is to be feared that very many in the church do not pray as much as they eat. They are not so frequent, nor so regular, and do not spend as much time.[16]

Finney never had a reputation for soft-pedaling the truth. Jesus very clearly taught that those who neglect the secret place of prayer are foolish because they have heard the call to pray but have chosen not to obey God's word. Obedient disciples who develop habits of secret prayer are wise, whereas those who hear the call but who consistently disobey are regarded as foolish. We are living in the day of the wise and foolish virgins. Jesus taught a parable later in the Gospel of Matthew that introduced the paradigm of bridal intimacy. We are clearly called to live within the revelation of the bridal paradigm. In this paradigm, Jesus revealed Himself as the Heavenly bridegroom, which automatically implies that His church is the bride.

We are living in a day where there is a clear prophetic call to the church to embrace the bridal paradigm. As God upgrades our revelation of Jesus as the Bridegroom King we automatically receive an upgrade in our self-perception of our bridal identity. God is calling us to embrace the call to be a bride that makes herself ready for the coming of the Bridegroom. Paul lived within this bridal paradigm in presenting Christ as the husband and the Church as His wife. "For this reason a man shall leave his father and mother and be joined to his wife, and the two shall become one flesh. This is a great mystery, but I speak concerning Christ and the church" (Ephesians 5:31-32). Paul said, "For I have betrothed you to one husband, that I may present you as a chaste virgin to Christ" (2 Corinthians 11:2).

Those who reject the call to the bridal paradigm will miss realms of experiential encounters with God. Those who pursue the intimate knowledge of Christ in the context of a corporate bride will be blessed in knowing Him as the Heavenly Bridegroom in a way that others simply cannot attain. In the Parable of the Wise and Foolish Virgins, Jesus taught His disciples an invaluable lesson concerning the cultivation of bridal intimacy. The wise virgins were those who kept their lamps trimmed and burning and filled with oil. The oil clearly spoke of the fullness of the Spirit and the heart connection of intimacy with the Heavenly Bridegroom.

At that time the kingdom of heaven will be like ten virgins who took their lamps and went out to meet the bridegroom. Five of them were foolish and five were wise. The foolish ones took their lamps but did not take any oil with them. The wise, however, took oil in jars along with their lamps. The bridegroom was a long time in coming, and they all became drowsy and fell asleep. At midnight the cry rang out: "Here's the bridegroom! Come out to meet him!" Then all the virgins woke up and trimmed their lamps. The foolish ones said to the wise, "Give us some of your oil; our lamps are going out." "No," they replied, "there may not be enough for both us and you. Instead, go to those who sell oil and buy some for yourselves." But while they were on their way to buy the oil, the bridegroom arrived. The virgins who were ready went in with him to the wedding banquet. And the door was shut. Later the others also came. "Sir! Sir!" they said, "Open the door for us!" But he replied, "I tell you the truth, I don't know you." "Therefore keep watch, because you do not know the day or the hour" (Matthew 25:1-13).

This parable is about being spiritually ready for the coming of the Bridegroom. The wise virgins had maintained a state of readiness for the Bridegroom, whereas the foolish virgins allowed their lamps to run out of oil. The oil in the lamp spoke of intimacy, and the point of the parable was that you couldn't borrow this oil from others. You have to "buy" oil for yourself by spending your precious time abiding in the presence of the Lord. It is only in this place where our hearts are refreshed and filled once again with that sense of intimacy with the Bridegroom who is the Lover of our souls. The wise virgins counseled the foolish virgins to "buy oil." It required an investment of time and energy to obtain this oil; it was not something that was transferable. It would be helpful for us to understand the historical and cultural background to the parable of the wise and foolish virgins in order to fully appreciate what Jesus was teaching His disciples.

Historically, there were three parts to a Jewish marriage in Jesus' day and each of these parts was quite different to our contemporary Western traditions of marriage.

1. The Selection of the Bride

Unlike our culture, the fathers of the bride and the groom arranged most ancient Jewish marriages. This initial stage in a new relationship amounted to a contract in which the couple to be married had little, if any, involvement with each other. The father of the bridegroom chose the bride. In the same way, our Heavenly Father has chosen us as a corporate bride for His Son, Jesus. "You are a chosen generation" (1 Peter 2:9)! Traditionally, the father of the bridegroom paid a price to the father of the bride.

2. Betrothal

The second stage was the *betrothal*. This was a traditional ceremony at which the bride and groom exchanged vows in the presence of family and friends. At that point the couple was considered formally married; their relationship could be broken only by a divorce, just as if they had been married for many years. However, in this stage of a Jewish marriage the couple was still forbidden to cohabit with one another. Mary and Joseph were in this state of betrothal when Mary became pregnant.

> Now the birth of Jesus Christ was as follows: when His mother Mary had been *betrothed* to Joseph, before they *came together* she was found to be with child by the Holy Spirit. Because Joseph her husband was a righteous man and did not want to expose her to public disgrace, he had in mind to *divorce* her quietly (Matthew 1:18-19).

At the betrothal the groom offered his bride a gift of value, a possession symbolic of his esteem for her and his willingness to sacrifice on her behalf. In the case of our Heavenly Bridegroom He gave the gift of laying down His life for us! "Husbands, love your wives, just as Christ also loved the church and *gave Himself* for her" (Ephesians 5:25). This was the ultimate betrothal gift! During the betrothal ceremony the groom made a ritual statement, such as the one found in Hosea 2:19–20, formally consecrating himself to his bride. "I will betroth you to Me forever; yes, I will betroth you to Me in righteousness and justice, in loving-kindness and mercy; I will betroth you to Me in faithfulness and you shall know the Lord."

The groom then poured a cup of wine for the prospective bride. Because Jewish law stated that a woman could not be forced to marry a man distasteful to her, the bride was ultimately allowed to choose whether to accept or reject the groom's proposal. If she drank the cup he offered, they were betrothed. On the night that Jesus was betrayed He offered the cup of wine to His disciples and they entered into a covenantal relationship with Him. "He also took the cup after supper, saying, "This cup is the new covenant in My blood, which is shed for you" (Luke 22:20).

If the husband happened to die during the betrothal, the bride was considered a widow although the marriage had not been physically consummated and the two had never lived together. The betrothal could last for many months, often up to a year, during which time the groom would establish himself in a business, trade, or farming and would make provision for a place for the couple to live. After Jesus entered into a covenant with His bride, He went away to prepare a place for her. "In My Father's house are many mansions; if it were not so, I would have told you. I go to prepare a place for you. And if I go and prepare a place for you, I will come again and receive you to Myself; that where I am, there you may be also" (John 14:2-3).

3. The Wedding Ceremony

At the end of the betrothal period the wedding feast would be held, and it was in the feast and its related celebrations that the entire community became involved. This festivity could last up to a week if the family was wealthy. It was at just such a community wedding in Cana that Jesus famously turned water into wine (all 185 gallons of it!). The entire community who attended the wedding feast to celebrate the impending union enjoyed the wine over a period of days. The festivities would begin with the groom's coming with his groomsmen to the bride's house, where her bridesmaids were waiting with her. It was customary to have ten bridesmaids who were the close friends of the bride.

As the time of the wedding approached, the bride and her sisters, cousins, and friends would wait together each evening in anticipation of the groom's arrival. It was customary for the groom to arrive suddenly, often later in the evening. The bridegroom and his friends would carry the bride through the streets to the wedding feast that was held at her new home in a jubilant procession accompanied by music, torches, and well wishers. The procession was generally conducted at night, and the wedding party used lamps or torches to illumine their way to the feast and to deliberately attract everyone's attention to the celebration.

At the wedding house, the bride and groom would each be dressed in white wedding garments, the color of purity. Then they would meet under the wedding canopy, which symbolized God's presence blessing their union. Finally, at the end of the feast period, a close friend of the groom, who acted much like a best man, would take the hand of the bride and place it in the hand of the groom, and the couple would be left alone for the first time together. The marriage would then be consummated and the couple would henceforth live together in their new home.

It was this third part of the Jewish marriage that Jesus used as the framework for the parable of the wise and foolish bridesmaids. Ever since the first coming of Jesus, we have been in the betrothal period awaiting the Bridegroom to come and receive His bride for the final physical consummation. The apostle Paul said, "For I am jealous for you with godly jealousy. For I have betrothed you to one husband, that I may present you as a chaste virgin to Christ" (2 Corinthians 11:2). Even though we are "betrothed" we are already married to Christ because we have entered into a covenant. Paul describes us as "married" to Christ in the book of Romans.

> For the woman who has a husband is bound by the law to her husband as long as he lives. But if the husband dies, she is released from the law of her husband. So then if, while her husband lives, she marries another man, she will be called an adulteress; but if her husband dies, she is free from that law, so that she is no adulteress, though she has married another man. Therefore, my brethren, you also have become dead to the law through the body of Christ, that you may be *married to another; to Him* who was raised from the dead, that we should bear fruit to God (Romans 7:2-4).

Nearly two thousand years ago, John was taken in a vision in the Spirit to see "the Lamb's wife." From this passage in Revelation, we learn that the Lamb's wife is a synonym for the bride. Through the lens of Jewish betrothal we understand that, as the bride of Christ corporately, we are already married to the Lord by covenant.

> Then one of the seven angels who had the seven bowls filled with the seven last plagues came to me and talked with me, saying, "Come, I will show you *the bride, the Lamb's wife.* And he carried me away in the Spirit to a great and high mountain, and showed me the great city, the holy Jerusalem, descending out of heaven from God, having the glory of God (Revelation 21:9-11).

The ten virgins (or bridesmaids) are a prophetic picture of the Church. These ten virgins represent the complete bride because biblically, ten is the number of completion. As we just read, Paul said that we are "chaste virgins" in our dedication to Christ. "For I have betrothed you to one husband that I may present you as a chaste virgin to Christ" (2 Corinthians 11:2). In the book of Revelation, John had a vision of the 144,000 (the church in her fullness). "These are the ones who were not defiled with women, for *they are virgins.* These are the ones who follow the Lamb wherever He goes. These were redeemed from among men, being first-fruits to God and to the Lamb" (Revelation 14:4). Virginity is a prophetic metaphor for purity and separation. A virgin has never consummated in marriage; therefore, she is pure and undefiled.

In the Parable of the Wise and Foolish Virgins, they all had lamps and they all had some oil, so they were all believers. But five virgins were wise and five were foolish. Jesus was teaching that as we await the final consummation, many in the church will lose sight of the bridal paradigm of intimacy and allows their lamp to run out of the oil of intimacy. The focus of the parable was clearly upon preparedness. The wise virgins maintained a state of readiness for the bridegroom, whereas the foolish virgins allowed their lamps to run out of oil.

It is difficult to escape the conclusion that the oil in the lamp represented a life of intimacy in the fullness of the Spirit. As we have already seen, you can't buy or borrow this oil from others. It is something you must procure for yourself at personal expense and inconvenience. The wise virgins counseled the foolish virgins to make haste and buy their own supply of oil. We are similarly counseled elsewhere in the Scriptures by Jesus to *buy* gold, wine, and milk.

> I counsel you to *buy from Me gold* refined in the fire, that you may be rich; and white garments, that you may be clothed, that the shame of your nakedness may not be revealed; and anoint your eyes with eye salve, that you may see (Revelation 3:18).

> Ho! Everyone who thirsts, come to the waters and you who have no money, come, buy and eat. Yes, come, *buy wine and milk* without money and without price (Isaiah 55:1).

We buy the oil of intimacy with God by spending time and energy investing our life into the secret place of intimate encounter. David refused to give anything to the Lord "that has cost me nothing!" (1 Chronicles 21:24 NLT). The gift of salvation is completely free, but the cultivation of deep intimacy with God is extremely costly; Jesus exhorts us to *count the cost*. God expects us to pay a price to build intimate friendship. The Christian who is not willing to make any kind of sacrifice to know God intimately sets himself up for mockery by the world because they began the Christian journey but were not able to master it.

> For which of you, intending to build a tower, does not sit down first and *count the cost*, whether he has enough to finish it; lest, after he has laid the foundation, and is not able to finish, all who see it begin to mock him, saying, "This man began to build and was not able to finish" (Luke 14:28-30).

Millions of Christians begin the journey with God but freak out when they realize it will actually cost them something. They are able to retain the semblance of a Christian life but all too often their unresolved heart issues come back to haunt them. Often, unbelievers will then mock and ridicule them because they were unable to overcome the very things they once denounced in others. We have to be willing to pay a price to live consistently with our confession as followers of Christ.

The Parable of the Wise and Foolish Virgins speaks powerfully about our heart relationship with our heavenly Bridegroom. It is a parable specifically about the heart and the quality of our heart relationship with the Lord. In his exceptional book, *Secrets of the Secret Place,* Bob Sorge writes:

> The wise came to buy oil for themselves in order to have a private burning heart relationship with the Lord. The oil of authentic relationship is bought at the cost of investing

time and energy in the secret place. The foolish will allow urgent matters of the moment to pull them away from the secret place after minimal infilling. The wise will stay and continue to be filled with oil until their hearts are energized by their love relationship with Jesus. When their foolishness becomes obvious, the foolish will turn to the wise and say, "Give us some of your oil!" They will recognize the wise have a depth in God that they never took the time and energy to cultivate.[17]

Jesus said to the foolish virgins, "I don't know you!" Here the Bridegroom King says to the foolish virgins that He has never enjoyed an intimate personal relationship with them. "The bridegroom came, and *those who were ready* went in with Him to the wedding feast; and the door was shut. Later the other virgins also came, saying, 'Lord, Lord, open up for us.' But He answered, 'Truly I say to you, I do not know you!'" (Matthew 25:10-12). The Bridegroom reluctantly says, "I do not have an intimate relationship with you so you cannot enter this wedding feast because it is a celebration of intimacy!" There are those in the church today who are filling their own lamps with the oil of intimacy and they are privileged to live in a place of spiritual preparedness in order to enter into the bridal feast.

It is important to note the distinction between what Jesus says in this parable to the foolish virgins and what He said to those in the Sermon on the Mount who cried "Lord, Lord" but who refused to do the will of God. To this latter company Jesus said, "I never knew you; depart from Me, you who practice lawlessness!" (Matthew 7:23). There is a distinction between those who were "virgins" but who had not cultivated the oil of intimacy and those who were unsaved and bound by lawlessness and rebellion. So, the Parable of the Wise and Foolish Virgins presents us with a picture of a company of intimate lovers of the Bridegroom juxtaposed against those who believed but had never invested themselves into developing an intimate relationship with the Bridegroom King. How many believers are there in the world who have no desire whatsoever to draw near to the Bridegroom in pursuit of deep spiritual intimacy? They are content to believe but they have no real heart to know God as intimate lovers.

The distinction in our parable is between those who were ready and those who were not. The theme of bridal readiness is found throughout the Scriptures. In the book of Revelation we read, "Let us be glad and rejoice and give Him glory, for the marriage of the Lamb has come, and His wife has made herself ready" (Revelation 19:7). In Ephesians we read, "That He might present her to Himself a glorious church, not having spot or wrinkle or any such thing, but that she should be holy and without blemish" (Ephesians 5:27). We are to be without spot or blemish. According to James, true spirituality is "to keep oneself unspotted from the world" (James 1:27).

The bride makes herself ready by keeping herself set apart to God from the defilement of this present evil world. She lives in the prophetic bridal paradigm of deepening intimacy. She invests her time into buying the oil of intimacy.

The entire bridal party has been invited to enter into the wedding feast of intimate celebration. But only those who have cultivated intimacy with the Bridegroom in the secret place enjoy the privilege of entering the corporate mystical feast. We can enter into the spirit of the wedding feast whenever our lamp is filled with the oil of intimacy. You can always tell those who are presently enjoying the wedding feast. They know how to engage their hearts with the Bridegroom and they are entranced by the glory of their Bridegroom King. The foolish virgins are continually distracted and looking around the room with a vacant stare because their hearts are not engaged with the Bridegroom. They haven't learned how to engage their heart in intimacy through beholding the glory of the Lord and gazing upon His beauty.

The Prophetic Significance of the Wedding Feast

Jesus promises to serve those who were dressed and ready for Him. In the following word picture Jesus again invokes the bridal paradigm by referencing the wedding banquet. Those whose lamps are trimmed and burning will enter into the banquet where Jesus Himself will present Himself as the Master of ceremonies and will serve the best wine to His wedding guests.

> Be dressed ready for service and keep your lamps burning, like men waiting for their master to return from a wedding banquet, so that when he comes and knocks they can immediately open the door for him. It will be good for those servants whose master finds them watching when he comes. I tell you the truth, he will dress himself to serve, will have them recline at the table and will come and wait on them. It will be good for those servants whose Master finds them ready, even if he comes in the second or third watch of the night (Luke 12:35-38 NIV).

There is an eschatological bridal feast that is about to take place. Jesus is coming again to return for His bride, and His second coming will be the final "consummation" where the bride and Bridegroom will be physically joined together for eternity. This event is described in the book of Revelation.

> And I heard, as it were, the voice of a great multitude, as the sound of many waters and as the sound of mighty thunderings, saying, "Alleluia! For the Lord God Omnipotent reigns! Let us be glad and rejoice and give Him glory, *for the marriage of the Lamb has come*, and His wife has made herself ready." And to her it was granted to be arrayed in fine linen, clean and bright, for the fine linen is the righteous acts of the saints. Then he said to me, "Write: 'Blessed are those who are called to the *marriage supper* of the Lamb!'" And he said to me, "These are the true sayings of God" (Revelation 19:6-9).

Because this eschatological wedding event is a heavenly reality that is celebrated in a dimension beyond the physical world, we the bride can enter into the spirit of the wedding feast whenever our lamp is filled with the oil of intimacy. Whenever the bride has made herself ready, she is eligible to enter into this spiritual wedding feast. The Bridegroom has prepared a place for us in the Spirit so that we can be with Him where He is in this present moment, not just when He returns at an unknown time in the future. Jesus lives in the perpetual celebration of the marriage supper (or the heavenly wedding feast) and we can enter this realm whenever we approach His throne in a state of spiritual readiness, filled with the revelation of the passion of our Bridegroom.

What if embedded deep within the expansive narrative of the Old and New Testament Scriptures there is a thread of revelation that can be woven together under the inspiration of the Spirit to reveal a unique dimension of spiritual blessing? This is a blessing that can only be experienced by the bride of Christ in this present age when she meets the criteria of a heart that values intimacy with the Bridegroom above everything this world has to offer. Jesus spoke of a company whom He called the "friends of the Bridegroom" (Matthew 9:15). They live within the wisdom of the bridal paradigm and have given their lives to serve the Bridegroom and His higher purposes as they relate to the bride. They are privy to a body of revelation that is hidden from the eyes of the foolish virgins who have rejected the wisdom of the intimacy paradigm.

These friends of the Bridegroom have the privilege to experience wonders and realities that are hidden from those who are satisfied with only shallow knowledge of heaven's deep reality. Like the ancient mystics, they have entered into the bliss and ecstasy of the future wedding feast and have tasted of the powers of the age to come. The parable of the wise and foolish virgins ushers us into this dimension of deep revelation that can only be appreciated by those who have immersed themselves into the bridal paradigm of mystical intimacy.

Jesus lives within this paradigm and He invites us to enter into the supreme joy of the mystical union between the bride and the Bridegroom. The Song of Songs carries the friends of the Bridegroom into this rich dimension of mystical union. It ushers them, through the Spirit of revelation, into the heights of ecstatic intimacy with the Bridegroom as they embrace the heart journey. They, along with the ancient mystics, will experience realms that can only be touched by lovesick worshippers. Song of Songs, written under inspiration by Solomon, contains the unique revelation of the wedding feast and the bridal chamber. It features the wise virgins as a corporate picture of the bride of Christ who have said yes to the intimacy paradigm.

> Let Him kiss me with the kisses of His mouth – for Your love is more delightful than wine! Pleasing is the fragrance of Your perfumes; Your name is like perfume poured out. No wonder the virgins love You! Take me away with You – let us hurry! Let the King bring me into His chambers. We rejoice and delight in You; we will praise Your love more than wine. How right they are to adore You (Song of Songs 1:2-4).

This bridal chamber is none other than the location of the heavenly wedding feast. The King brings His bride into this secret place of bridal intimacy and lavishes His love upon His bride. "He brought me to the banqueting house and His banner over me was love" (Song of Songs 2:4). This *banqueting house* is the *yayin bayith*, or the *house of wine*, in the Hebrew text. In this place, Jesus assumes the role of humble servant, serving His bride the mystical wine of His love, intoxicating her with the ecstasy of His incomparable love. The Bridegroom Himself promised that He would serve those wise virgins who have made themselves ready. "I tell you the truth, He will dress Himself to serve, will have them recline at the table and will come and wait on them." As we gaze into the Scriptures we see various passages, appearing almost randomly, awaiting the friends of the Bridegroom to weave them together into a rich revelatory tapestry. Solomon's father, David, touched this heavenly vineyard of revelation when he wrote:

The King's daughter is all glorious within; her clothing is interwoven with gold. She shall be brought to the King in robes of many colors; the virgins, her companions who follow her, shall be brought to You. What a joyful, enthusiastic procession as they enter the King's palace (Psalm 45:13-15 NKJV/NLT)!

This passage reminds us of Matthew 25 with the story of the torch-lit procession of the virgins as they make their way to the bridal chamber. The wise virgins are ushered into the royal palace and are seated to feast at the table with the King. The King Himself promised those who heard His voice and who opened the door to Him that, "I will come in, and we will share a meal as friends" (Revelation 3:20 NLT). The Bridegroom serves the bride and says, "Eat, O friends, and drink; drink your fill, O lovers" (Song of Songs 5:1 NIV). The Hebrew word for *drink your fill* is s*hakar,* which literally means to *be made drunk*. It is within the King's chamber that the bride is deeply intoxicated and overtaken by the wine of intimacy. This wine makes the heart of the lover of God completely ecstatic. And in this experience of bridal ecstasy the Spirit of revelation is poured out in much greater measure.

Five of Them Were Wise

In the Parable of the Wise and Foolish Virgins, five of them were foolish because they didn't invest themselves into the intimate knowledge of the heart of their Bridegroom. The call to the wedding feast is universal, but entry to the wedding feast is definitely conditional.

The Kingdom of Heaven can be illustrated by the story of a King who prepared a great wedding feast for his Son. Many guests were invited, and when the banquet was ready, He sent his servants to notify everyone that it was time to come. But they all refused (Matthew 22:2-3 NLT)!

Jesus concludes this parable by saying, "For many are called, but few are chosen" (Matthew 22:14). Experience in church life tells us that some who are invited refuse to accept the invitation, but those who accept are chosen, and are thus entitled to enter into the mystical wedding feast. As we have seen, Jesus said to the church, "Behold, I stand at the door and knock; if anyone hears My voice and opens the door, I will come in to him and will dine with him, and he with Me" (Revelation 3:20). This is the Bridegroom's invitation to enter the mystic wedding feast: the *banqueting house* or the *house of wine*! (Song of Songs 2:4). But we must hear and obey by opening the door. If we hesitate and resist the invitation, we can miss our window of opportunity. "Seek the Lord while He may be found; call upon Him while He is near" (Isaiah 55:6).

The Bridegroom draws near and invites us to enter into a dimension of intimate encounter. In the Song of Songs, the Bridegroom comes to the bride but she hesitates because she rationalizes in her mind rather than responding from her heart.

> I sleep, but my heart is awake; it is the voice of my Beloved! He knocks, saying, "Open for Me, My sister, My love, My dove, My perfect one; For My head is covered with dew, My locks with the drops of the night." I have taken off my robe; how can I put it on again? I have washed my feet; how can I defile them? My Beloved put His hand by the latch of the door and my heart yearned for Him (Song of Songs 5:2-4).

Did Jesus have this passage of Scripture in mind when He spoke the Parable of the Wise and Foolish Virgins? The bride went through a series of rationalizations in her mind. She had already taken a bath and if she went outside in response to the voice of the Bridegroom, her feet might get dirty! She had already put on her night attire and if she stepped out the door she might be seen in her underwear! Eventually, she roused herself to respond to the Bridegroom only to discover that she had missed her window of opportunity. "I opened to my Beloved, but my Beloved had turned away and had gone! My heart went out to Him as He spoke. I searched for Him but I did not find Him; *I called Him but He did not answer me*" (Song of Songs 5:6).

This scenario forms the backdrop of the Parable of the Wise and Foolish Virgins. The five foolish virgins similarly missed their window of opportunity because they hesitated. They had run out of the oil that serves as a potent symbol of intimacy. They realized their folly but it was too late. They pleaded with the Bridegroom to enter the wedding feast but they were refused admission. This may seem unfair to some but they cannot claim that they were not informed or repeatedly invited.

Like the bride in the Song of Songs, we need to constantly guard our hearts against the paralysis of analysis. In this mystical song we are given a glimpse into a heart that became entangled in rational lies as the one who was being romanced began to rationalize about the call to a deeper intimacy. How many believers hear the voice of the Bridegroom but get stuck in their heads, trapped in theology instead of responding from the heart? This is the great battle for intimacy that every single believer must face. Unfortunately, so much of the church in the Western world has been ensnared in the Greek focus of rationalism and intellectualism. Jesus is seeking to romance His bride, but the church has lost its way in an intellectual response. The bride struggles because so often managers, instead of mystics, are leading the church!

The key to the King's bridal chamber is the deliberate cultivation of a lifestyle of intimacy. The Bridegroom calls us again and again, but if we repeatedly refuse to respond, we ought not be surprised if we call and He doesn't respond! "When I called, you did not answer; when I spoke, you did not hear" (Isaiah 65:12). "I spoke to you, rising up early and speaking, but you did not hear, and I called you but you did not answer" (Jeremiah 7:13). "They made their hearts as hard as flint and would not listen to the words that the Lord Almighty had sent by his Spirit through the earlier prophets. *"When I called, they did not listen; so when they called, I would not listen,"* says the Lord Almighty" (Zechariah 7:12-13).

The five foolish virgins did not respond to the call of the Bridegroom, so when they called out to Him the Bridegroom did not respond to them! Many are called to bridal intimacy but few are chosen to enter into the mystical wedding feast. God repeatedly calls us but when we refuse to listen we invariably continue on a course that consolidates us in our stubbornness. A persistent lifestyle of resistance to the call to seek the Lord establishes us in patterns of spiritual obstinacy. How many believers are still deepening this stronghold of an obstinate heart that refuses the call to intimacy? Jesus lamented this great obstinacy when He famously spoke those tear-filled words over the city of the great King.

> O Jerusalem, Jerusalem, the one who kills the prophets and stones those who are sent to her! How often I wanted to gather your children together, as a hen gathers her chicks under her wings, *but you were not willing* (Matthew 23:37)!

This pattern of chronic unwillingness to respond to the call to intimacy renders the people of God foolish. Jesus clearly didn't anticipate universal willingness amongst His people in their response to the call to intimacy, even though He invites each of us day and night to embrace the intimacy paradigm. Wisdom cries out to us to respond to the call to seek the Bridegroom!

> Wisdom shouts in the streets. She cries out in the public square. She calls out to the crowds along the main street, and to those in front of city hall. "You simpletons!" she cries. "How long will you go on being simpleminded? How long will you mockers relish your mocking? How long will you fools fight the facts? Come here and listen to me! I will pour

out the spirit of wisdom upon you and make you wise. I called you so often, but you didn't come. I reached out to you, but you paid no attention. You ignored my advice and rejected the correction I offered" (Proverbs 1:20-25 NLT).

I will not answer when they cry for help. Even though they anxiously search for me, they will not find me. For they hated knowledge and chose not to fear the Lord. They rejected my advice and paid no attention when I corrected them. That is why they must eat the bitter fruit of living their own way (Proverbs 1:28-31 NLT).

God seeks to train our hearts in the art of mystical encounter! The wise virgins have learnt how to engage their hearts in intimacy with God. The foolish virgins stand in the midst of the wedding feast and look lost and disengaged. It is as though they are living in another dimension. One saint can be caught up in mystical rapture, intoxicated by the love of Christ whilst another believer, standing right next to them in a worship gathering, may appear totally disengaged and oblivious the presence of the King of glory. The invitation to intimacy comes inconveniently in the midst of our busyness. Even in the midst of the busyness of serving Jesus, we can run out of the oil of intimacy. This was the condition of the saints in Ephesus, only some thirty years after the great revival recorded in the Book of Acts that centered around this city.

To the angel of the church in Ephesus write: These are the words of Him who holds the seven stars in His right hand and walks among the seven golden lamp-stands: I know your deeds, your *hard work* and your perseverance. I know that you cannot tolerate wicked men, that you have tested those who claim to be apostles but are not, and have found them false. You have persevered and have endured hardships for My name, and have not grown weary. Yet I hold this against you: *You have forsaken your first love.* Remember the height from which you have fallen! Repent and do the things you did at first. If you do not repent, I will come to you and remove your lamp-stand from its place (Revelation 2:1-5, 7 NIV).

The lamp-stand represents the oil of intimate first love. It illuminates our hearts and it guides our path in the intimate knowledge of God. The Bridegroom is deeply grieved when we forsake the bridal paradigm and become Marthas instead of Marys. That is why He calls us to repentance! Only heartfelt repentance paves the way for the restoration of our first love relationship with Jesus. When we come into the secret place, we enter into a spirit of repentance. There are many subtle attitudes and lies that we need to repent of in the presence of the Lord. Isaiah taught us that God dwells with the contrite of heart. Contrition paves the way for true intimacy with God.

> For thus says the High and Lofty One who inhabits eternity, whose name is Holy: "I dwell in the high and holy place with him who has a contrite and humble spirit, to revive the spirit of the humble and to revive the heart of the contrite ones." (Isaiah 57:15)

In his devotional masterpiece, *Secrets of the Secret Place,* Bob Sorge writes:

> *Prayer is the constant calibration of the soul.* It is a lifestyle of stopping and taking candid spiritual inventory. This is not spiritual paranoia, but rather the exercise of one who has a healthy fear of God and a sublime desire for glorious heights of intimacy with God. The devout is constantly testing himself for spiritual fervor, alertness, faithfulness, purity, love, obedience, growth in grace, etc. It is in the secret place that I find "my spirit makes diligent search" (Psalm 77:6). I so very much long to please Him and to know His will, so my spirit diligently searches the recesses of my heart to see if there

might be anything in me for which I need to repent. I want nothing of my self-life to hinder my relationship with Him or His purposes for us together. I feel like I'm panning for gold—the finds are few and not as weighty as I would desire. Here's some excellent counsel: *Become a good repenter.* The only way to move forward in God is through repentance. If your pride hinders you from repenting, get over it.[18]

The wise virgins continue to say yes to the call to repentance and a life of obedient prayer; they relentlessly press in to the place of intimate first love for Jesus. The foolish virgins hear the same call but harden their hearts to the voice of the Bridegroom as they descend into an intellectual, theological response. We as the corporate church need a healthy dose of repentance that calls us away from our intellectual pride and back to a heart response of intimacy. One of the most significant decisions we will ever make as followers of Jesus is what we choose to do with the intimacy paradigm. Every single day of our lives we are faced with a choice: do we humble ourselves and respond to the romantic overtures of a lovesick Bridegroom, or do we embrace an intellectual faith that stays locked into the mind rather than the heart?

Follow the Worshippers!

Who are the people in the church that are seeking to live from the heart? How do we connect ourselves with a company of believers who will keep us accountable to get on the heart journey of intimacy with God and stay there? We are all looking for role models and mentors. The Lord once spoke to me and said, "Follow the worshippers!" They are the ones who continually rend their hearts before God, seeking to maintain the fire of first love. The very act of worship is a heart response to God. God doesn't want people to draw near with their lips when their hearts are far from Him. That is why the Father is seeking true heart worshippers. Jesus said:

A time is coming and has now come when the true worshipers will worship the Father in spirit and truth, for they are the kind of worshipers the Father seeks. God is spirit, and his worshipers must worship in spirit and in truth (John 4:23-24 NIV).

The Father constantly searches for true worshippers who know how to rend their hearts in order to press into the Secret Place of intimate encounter. God desires truth in the heart. "Behold, You desire truth in the inward parts and in the hidden part You will make me to know wisdom" (Psalm 51:6). This is the wisdom of the worshipper. The wise virgins are worshippers who recalibrate their hearts on a daily basis in order to keep their hearts tender and soft toward the Lover of their souls. They refuse to step out of the intimacy paradigm, even for a day, because they know how readily the world hardens them to the heart of God. I love the *New Living Translation* of Psalm 51:6: "You desire honesty from the heart so you can teach me to be wise in my inmost being." The Father seeks worshippers who rend their heart and not their outer garments. "For the eyes of the Lord move to and fro throughout the earth that He may strongly support those whose heart is completely His" (2 Chronicles 16:9 NASB). Bowing down before the Lord in true heart-felt worship is the beginning of wisdom.

The worship songs that impact and stir my heart the most probe this dimension of living from the heart, where truth and wisdom are valued as costly pearls. One such song is *You Won't Relent* by Misty Edwards. This song is an absolute favorite of mine because it so beautifully focuses upon the simplicity of heart devotion to God and the cry for the fire of God's love to burn powerfully inside of us.

There is so much glory on this song, which is framed within the context of Song of Songs 8:6-7.

You wont relent until you have it all, my heart is Yours.

I'll set You as a seal upon my heart, as a seal upon my arm

For there is love that is as strong as death, jealousy demanding as the grave
And many waters cannot quench this love.
Come be the fire inside of me, come be the flame upon my heart
Come be the fire inside of me, until You and I are one.

The best worship songs are ones that probe and stir the heart to a genuine vertical response, not necessarily the ones that include the word "heart." Worship is the most heavenly activity we can ever engage in this side of heaven. There is an invisible feast set apart for those who approach the Father and the Son with a true heart of worship. I have purposed to immerse myself in a worshipping community all the days of my life because I recognize the power of the spirit of the world to pull me out of true worship and into idolatry. I don't want to be in a place where I end up worshipping something other than the one true God.

Every human being is a worshipper by nature. The question is: who or what will we worship? Worshipping God day and night keeps us safe from the lure of idolatry; it deepens our intimacy with God until it becomes a stronghold of safety in our hearts. The intimacy paradigm leads us inexorably to the heart of true worship where we eat the invisible feast of the glory of the Lord. It's a safe addiction, so follow the worshippers!

Part Two

Supernatural Heart Transformation

In part two, we explore the contemporary anti-supernatural challenge that has arisen within the church. These beliefs hinder the restoration of a widespread revelation of the supernatural transformation of the heart. Jesus taught us to pray for His kingdom to come on earth, just as it is in heaven. Biblical theology intentionally juxtaposes that which is from above with that which is of the earth. "He who comes from above is above all; he who is of the earth is earthly and speaks of the earth" (John 3:31). James contrasted the "wisdom that is from above" with a wisdom that "does not descend from above" (James 3:15,16). He concluded that, "Every good and perfect gift is from above" (James 1:17 NIV). There is a spiritual battle raging within the church between a model of heart transformation that is exclusively from above and a model that leans on natural earthly wisdom and techniques. We conclude our study with a prophetic call to recover the fullness of the supernatural paradigm of heart transformation pioneered by Jesus. This paradigm has largely been eclipsed by a non-supernatural model that is centred in "talk therapy" instead of the transformation that comes through encountering the glory and power of God.

Chapter Nine

Secular Psychology and the Knowledge of the Heart

Rick had been a Christian for thirty-two years but his marriage was in deep trouble. His wife had been threatening divorce for the past three years because of Rick's addiction to pornography and his struggle to give up smoking. He knew he needed help but all his pastor could do was to encourage him to keep on repenting. His job repairing computers placed him within continuous reach of the very thing that was destroying his marriage. Eventually, a friend recommended that he visit a local psychologist in his quest to get to the root of his addictive personality. His psychologist was expensive but he really didn't want to lose his wife and end up a lonely old man.

Dr. Morris had a great deal of insight into the human personality and addictive disorders but Rick was confused by his repeated reference to the "unconscious mind." He was told that there were unconscious forces at work deep within him that relentlessly drove him into addictive patterns of behavior. This resonated with him because he knew there was a lot going on inside of him that he didn't understand. Yet, he recalled someone in the church telling him that the concept of the unconscious mind was not biblically based. Meanwhile his addiction grew stronger and stronger the more he ignored the conviction of the Holy Spirit.

Dr. Morris also recommended hypnotherapy to gain a deeper understanding of the roots of his addictive personality, but Rick was not inclined to allow himself to be hypnotized by Dr. Morris. When he asked his pastor about hypnotherapy, he was warned that this would not be a good practice to submit to because of the risk of demonic influence while he was in a hypnotized state. Rick was desperate, but now he was completely confused.

The industry of secular psychology needs to be applauded for their tireless commitment to helping people overcome personal problems of living. Psychology is an extremely broad field of study that has produced countless helpful insights into the human condition. Psychology is the study of the soul, which includes the intellectual, emotional, and volitional dimensions of human existence. Neuropsychology has also given us tremendous insights into the function of the brain. As a broad field of study, psychology has made some tremendous contributions to our knowledge of the human condition.

Much of psychology is theologically neutral. The scientific and empirical study of the human mind, human emotions, and patterns of behavior offer us insights and understanding that do not impinge negatively upon biblical theology. For example, the study of emotional intelligence, neuroscience, and the observation of personality types and personality profiling do not detract from our biblical understanding of human beings. In many positive ways these insights add to our understanding of people.

But for the Christian, when psychologists seek to define the human personality by proposing theories that contradict biblical concepts they are treading on dangerous ground. One example of this is the idea of the unconscious mind. This concept has caused many Christians a lot of confusion. No study of the theme of the revelatory knowledge of the heart would be complete without engaging in a biblical evaluation of the teaching of the unconscious mind. The concept of the unconscious mind is the secular counterpart to the biblical concept of the *hidden person of the heart*.

Secular Psychology and the Knowledge of the Heart

Let me tell you right up front that I do not buy into the concept of the unconscious mind. I am in full agreement that there definitely are *unconscious forces* within our hearts that motivate us to do things that are against our better judgment. On this point, I agree with secular psychologists. But I have found that although there are some similarities between the secular concept of an unconscious mind and the biblical concept of the hidden person of the heart, there are significant distinctions that need to be made that are more than mere semantics.

As I have studied this subject, I have found that the concept of the unconscious mind is not in harmony with biblical revelation. The adoption of this concept into the practice of Christian counselling actually undermines the unveiling of the supernatural ministry of Jesus. The introduction of this concept into counselling is presented as a worthy supplement to biblical counselling practice. But anything that we seek to add to the ministry of Jesus actually ends up subtracting from the revelation of the fullness of His ministry. I once heard a preacher say, "Jesus plus nothing equals everything!" Whenever we seek to supplement the ministry of Jesus with an extra-biblical concept, that concept ends up becoming the unique ministry *distinctive* that eclipses the unveiling of Christ's kingdom ministry.

Remember that the prophetic knowledge of the heart is founded upon the revelation of the sufficiency of Christ and His Word, coupled with the reality that there is only one true ministry: the perfect ministry of Jesus. Our sole responsibility is to receive His ministry into our hearts and then to participate with Christ in extending His supernatural ministry into other people's lives. The suggestion that the perfect ministry of Jesus needs to be supplemented with extra-biblical concepts actually tells us more about the person who believes that the ministry of Jesus needs some kind of secular augmentation. The transformational ministry of Christ is a supernatural ministry. It is established upon the application of the unlimited resources of heaven to the lives of those who are seeking spiritual freedom.

A survey of much of the contemporary Christian literature currently available on the subject of Christian psychology and counselling reveals that a significant number of theories and concepts that have their origin in secular psychology have gradually crept into Christianity. These ideas have had a considerable influence upon the language and ideas that have come to characterise the Christian counselling movement. One of the most widely accepted assumptions among those who advocate the integration of Christianity and psychology is the alleged existence of the "unconscious mind."

The concept of the unconscious mind has its origin in the theories of the secular psychologist, Sigmund Freud. There are those Christian counsellors who warmly embrace this concept, and there are others who counsel us to proceed with great caution in the whole area of the integration of Christianity with psychology. One such author is Ed Bulkley. In his book *Why Christians Can't Trust Psychology*, he outlines the development of the concept of the unconscious mind:

> In Freud's system, the mind is comprised of three distinct areas: the conscious (thoughts, concepts, and ideas a person is aware of), the preconscious (ideas that are not in the forefront of one's mind but can easily be drawn out by an act of the will), and the unconscious (ideas a person cannot be aware of due to repression). Carl Jung expanded the concept of the unconscious to include not only one's own past but also one's collective ancestral past. Is Freud's theory of the unconscious a scientifically proven fact? No, but it is a sociological belief so deeply ingrained in our culture that society accepts the concept without question.[19]

Not only does modern Western culture accept the existence of the unconscious mind as if it was a scientifically proven fact, a considerable portion of the evangelical church unquestioningly embraces this popular tenet of secular psychology. The *Dictionary of Pastoral Care* defines the unconscious mind as "that part of the mind or psyche containing information that has never been conscious, or that was once conscious but is no longer."[20] The dictionary article states that Sigmund Freud,

> ... emphasized that although various thoughts and experiences are excluded from consciousness, this material nevertheless exerts important influences upon conscious life and behavior. Freud and his disciples employed techniques such as hypnosis, free association, dream analysis, and projective testing to uncover unconscious psychological processes, and based psychoanalytic therapy upon the skilled interpretation of these materials. By gaining awareness of disruptive processes within the unconscious, patients could be helped to achieve emotional resolutions to their problems.[21]

Because many in the field of Christian counselling have uncritically embraced the concept of the unconscious mind without subjecting it to biblical scrutiny, these counsellors have also embraced a number of secular techniques to try to "access" the unconscious mind. For example, it is not at all uncommon to find hypnotherapy practiced in some Christian counselling practices. Some Christians are alarmed when they hear that a form of secular hypnotism is employed by Christian counsellors to dredge up the contents of the unconscious mind, whereas other Christians have become powerful advocates of hypnotherapy as a tool to access areas of the mind that are shut down due to repressed memories.

I was personally quite disturbed to learn that the counselling department of a Christian ministry training college that I was enrolled in practiced hypnotherapy. Where a Christian stands on the issue of hypnotherapy in the church will be determined largely by the degree of revelation that person has (or doesn't have) concerning the "heaven to earth" model of ministry revealed by Jesus. I cannot in my wildest dreams imagine Jesus adopting such a practice! The adoption of techniques such as hypnotherapy are rooted in the commitment to the concept of the unconscious mind.

Larry Crabb, a leading Christian psychologist, was so convinced of the necessity of integrating the concept of the unconscious with the Bible that he argued that a Christian counsellor who is not equipped with an understanding of the unconscious will be largely ineffective in ministering to those who seek pastoral help. Because of his commitment to the concept of the unconscious mind, Crabb believed that secular psychotherapists, armed with an understanding of the unconscious, are better equipped to heal than Christian counsellors who are not.

> When a psychologist refers to the idea of an unconscious, many evangelicals quickly assume that his secular training is having a stronger influence on his thinking than the teachings of Scripture. Because Freud was the first to systematise and emphasise how unconscious forces affect behavior, it is commonly accepted that the idea is more psychiatric than theological. As a result, while the church exhorts people to do what they consciously know to do, psychotherapists deal with the casualties of the church: people who sense that mysterious forces within are frustrating their efforts to obey.[22]

> Unless we understand sin as rooted in unconscious beliefs and motives and figure out how to expose and deal with these deep forces within the personality, the church will continue to promote superficial adjustment while psychotherapists, with or without biblical foundations, will do a better job than the church of restoring troubled people to more effective functioning. And that is a pitiful tragedy.[23]

This is a very strong claim. Remember that secular psychotherapists do not understand the new creation or the power of the blood of Jesus to cleanse the heart of all unrighteousness. Larry Crabb actually suggested that Christians who are ignorant of the existence of the unconscious mind are less equipped than a secular psychotherapist who does not even counsel from a biblical foundation or who does not have a grasp of our new nature in Christ. This is unwarranted intimidation that appears to be designed to rob non-professional Christian counsellors from their confidence in the sufficiency of Christ in the field of counselling.

Crabb may have changed his position since these rather extreme statements written in his earlier books. In fairness to him, he has shifted further away from his militant integrationist posture as the years have progressed and as his own thinking has been shaped more and more by biblical revelation. Nevertheless, many in the field of Christian counselling embrace the integrationist sentiments he once expressed. We will explore the arguments for and against integrationism in the next chapter.

Almost without exception all Christian counsellors and psychotherapists who advocate the integration of psychotherapy and Christianity regard the modern "scientific" discovery of the unconscious mind as the key to emotional, psychological, and spiritual well-being. But the question must be asked: is this a biblical concept and is it consistent with the biblical view of human nature? Does the concept of the unconscious mind *supplement* the revelation of human nature given in the Scriptures, or does it inadvertently distort it?

Developing a Biblical Anthropology

The revelation of the nature of God is the most appropriate starting point in developing a biblical understanding of human nature, because all human beings have been made in God's image. If men and women are truly made in the image and likeness of God (Genesis 1:26-27), then our understanding of the nature of God is foundational to a correct understanding of human nature. Jesus declared, "God is spirit" (John 4:24), which essentially means that

God is a spiritual being. Humans are also described as spiritual beings. Paul spoke of "the spirit of a man" (1 Corinthians 2:11), and James said, "The body without the spirit is dead" (James 2:26).

God also has a heart. Many places in the Bible we read about the heart of God, "The Lord was sorry that he had made man on the earth, and he was grieved in *His heart*" (Genesis 6:6). God described David as "a man after *My own heart*" (Acts 13:22). Because humans are made in God's image, we also have a heart. As we have already seen, there are almost a thousand references to the heart in the Bible. Some of these refer to the heart of God, but the vast majority refer to the human heart.

God also describes Himself as having a soul. For example, in Jeremiah we read, "Yes, I will rejoice over them to do them good and I will plant them in this land, with all My heart and *all My soul*" (Jeremiah 32:41). Not surprisingly, when God made us in His own image we also became a "living soul" (Genesis 2:7). The conventional theological understanding of the term soul is that it constitutes the mind, the will, and the emotions of a person. It follows that if God describes Himself as having a soul, then He has a mind, a will, and emotions.

As we might expect, the Bible is replete with references to the mind of God, thoughts of God, will of God, and emotions of God. In fact, a study of the emotional life of God the Father and Jesus the Son is quite a revelation in itself. God has a broad spectrum of emotions, though He is never controlled by them as humans sometimes are. Nevertheless, God clearly has feelings toward others, and these feelings are often quite strong!

Like our Creator, we are self-conscious, personal beings with all the attributes of personhood. Human beings are an exact replication of God's personhood, but in a *finite* form. God revealed Himself to Moses as "I AM" (Exodus 3:14). Yet man, as a living, thinking personality can also say, "I am!" As Descartes, the French philosopher said, "I think, therefore *I am!*" I think God was the first one to say that. The essence of "personhood" is that we each possess an intelligent consciousness of our own existence. As spiritual beings made in the image and likeness of God, we have a staggering capacity to think, create, and communicate with one another at a profoundly complex level. We have the ability to choose, feel, and enjoy spiritual fellowship with our Creator. The human being is the crowning achievement of God's intelligent and creative design.

We began this inquiry by asking if the concept of the unconscious mind was biblical. The answer to this question lies in the fact that we are made in the image and likeness of God. Does God have an unconscious mind? If He does, then it follows that those who are created in His image also do. Yet the very thought of the all-knowing God being in some way ignorant of His own inner thought processes blatantly contradicts the concept of divine omniscience. The suggestion that humans simultaneously have both a conscious and an unconscious mind is clearly not founded on biblical revelation.

But some may argue: what if a part of our thought processes became *unconscious* at the fall? The problem here is that secular psychologists do not have a paradigm for the fall. They assert that the unconscious mind is a constant existential reality with absolutely no reference to people undergoing some kind of quantum spiritual degradation in their earlier collective history. Christian psychologists could perhaps get a lot of mileage out of integrating the biblical doctrine of the fall with the emergence of the unconscious mind. However, it would still take us away from a purely biblical nomenclature and a biblical understanding of human nature.

There are clearly mysterious forces at work within us that thwart our noblest intentions. But this force is not that of the "unconscious mind," rather it is the unknowable heart with its sinful motives and desires that wage war against everything that human beings know to be righteous and good. The sinful heart of fallen men and women continually thwarts the noblest intentions of the mind. All educated people know that such things as war, crime, oppression, theft, pedophilia, sex trafficking, and abuse are wrong but our best efforts, both personally and collectively, to eradicate these problems through education have failed miserably.

How often do people intend to be kind but always end up hurting others with their words or their actions? Marriage is the perfect example. When a couple enter into a marriage covenant they solemnly vow to love and to cherish one another, yet approximately half of all marriages end in painful divorce. Nobody ever enters marriage with the intention of breaking the heart of the one they love! The same principle applies to parenting. What parent has children with the express purpose of abusing them and destroying their lives? (Unless they are deeply twisted satanists.) Yet how many children have been deeply wounded by well-intentioned parents who ended up rejecting or abusing their own children?

Paul described this continual conflict between the noblest intentions of the mind and the sinful condition of the heart in Romans chapter seven. As a Jew who had received a revelation of God's will through the law of Moses, his complaint was that:

> With the mind I myself serve the law of God.... But I see another law in my members, warring against the law of my mind, and bringing me into captivity to the law of sin which is in my members (Romans 7:23, 25).

> For what I am doing, I do not understand. For what I will to do that I do not practice; but what I hate, that I do. If, then, I do what I will not to do, I agree with the law that it is good. But now, it is no longer I who do it, but sin that dwells in me. For I know that in me (that is, in my flesh) nothing good dwells; for to will is present with me, but how to perform

what is good I do not find. For the good that I will to do, I do not do; but the evil I will not to do, that I practice. Now if I do what I will not to do, it is no longer I who do it, but sin that dwells in me. I find then a law, that evil is present with me, the one who wills to do good (Romans 7:15-21).

Paul was deeply aware of mysterious forces that were at work within him, which thwarted his best cognitive intentions to please God. If we were to ask Paul to describe this mysterious force within us, he would explain to us the reality of the sinful condition of the fallen human heart. Then he would proceed to point us to the redemptive power of the blood of Christ to renew our hearts. The unconscious mind cannot be cleansed; it can only—in theory—be *re-programmed* through expensive psychotherapy. Even then, there is no way of assessing whether it has been sufficiently re-programmed.

The ultimate "unconscious force" in the human heart is sin, but regrettably, secular psychologists do not have a paradigm for sin. They sometimes even consider this idea to be the very source of unhealthy feelings of guilt, imposed upon the populace by fundamentalist religion. To the extent that anybody seeks to side step the biblical unveiling of sin, to that same extent they will need to find an alternative explanation to account for these apparent unconscious forces at work within the human personality. This highlights the absolute importance of embracing strictly biblical nomenclature.

God's answer to the human predicament is not subliminal re-programming, but the power of the cross. God is not seeking the *changed* life; He seeks the *exchanged* life, and this is only accomplished through the work of the cross. He does not seek to tweak or adjust the unrenewed nature; He seeks to completely put it to death! Here the whole concept of the unconscious mind collapses in a heap; it is not part of the biblical revelation of human nature.

Therefore, whenever someone embraces this secular concept and seeks to heal broken people they will always be working with a model that is fundamentally flawed, They will inevitably adopt therapeutic practices that violate the biblical process of renewing and transforming the hidden person of the heart; a process that is grounded firmly upon the foundation of the new creation miracle. What begins as a well-intentioned endeavour to supplement and improve upon Christian ministry ends up significantly diminishing and undermining the supernatural ministry of Christ.

For those of us who seek to work with broken people, we need to exercise considerable caution in the development of our theory of the human personality. If we seek to integrate secular concepts with the biblical theory of the human personality, it will have a domino effect all the way down the line in the nature of our ministry to broken people. And to the extent to which we deviate away from an exclusively biblical understanding of the human condition, to that same extent we will deviate away from a solidly biblical outcome in our ministry. If this is true, every church should tread extremely carefully in adopting models of ministry that extol the virtues of integrationism. The kind of ministry model that a church adopts in the field of personal transformation actually becomes a litmus test of the level of revelation they have received concerning the "heaven to earth" model espoused by Jesus.

The development of the idea of an unconscious mind was nothing more than the unenlightened speculation of a person who sought to understand human nature apart from the revelation of Scripture. Freud's psychological speculations developed on the assumption that the biblical revelation of human nature was irrelevant to any serious discussion about the real problems faced by real people. Though he was raised in a Jewish home, he had no time for the faith of his fathers. Despite his rejection of biblical revelation, Freud had an intense desire to understand human nature. Thus, he became the father of the popular theory that an unconscious part of the human mind controls behavior.

Freud was an atheist who openly rejected the biblical concept of God as the One who punished those who were guilty of sin. Freedom from guilt is a recurring theme in Freud's psychotherapy. The presence of a deep, inner sense of guilt for "sinful" acts or thoughts was itself considered by Freud to be an obstacle to personal wholeness and well-being. Freud came to consider "the obstacle of an unconscious sense of guilt ... as the most powerful of all obstacles to recovery."[24]

Freud did not turn a blind eye to the evils of humanity but he refused to embrace the sin/guilt paradigm. Had Freud embraced the Bible and submitted his mind to the renewing power of the Word of God, he would have inevitably come to a revelation of the sinful depravity of the human heart out of which flows all kinds of evil thoughts and bizarre behavior. Jesus plainly taught that, "Out of the heart proceed evil thoughts, murders, adulteries, fornications, thefts, false witness, and blasphemies" (Matthew 15:19). It is this reality that Jesus purposes to "put to death" through the power of the cross. Relentlessly dredging up unconscious forces through such techniques as hypnotherapy becomes a poor replacement for the wisdom and power of the cross!

Freud was right on one important point; he was profoundly aware that there are motives, desires, and hidden factors that drive people to do bizarre and inexplicable things, often against their own better judgment. But because his own understanding was darkened (Ephesians 4:18) due to his own rejection of God, he attributed these actions to the existence of an "unconscious mind." Had he thought in biblical terms and adopted biblical nomenclature, he would have come to appreciate that human beings, in their fallen and unenlightened state, are entirely ignorant of the *sinful* condition of their own heart. The real issue is the widespread ignorance of the reality of the sinful nature of humanity.

Paul attributed this ignorance to the hardness of our hearts toward God. "They are darkened in their understanding and separated from the life of God because of the ignorance that is in them due to the hardening of their hearts" (Ephesians 4:18 NIV). Whenever we reject divine revelation, we voluntarily lose touch with reality. As a result, "all a man's ways seem innocent to him" (Proverbs 16:2). In other words, we continually exonerate ourselves of blame and place the blame upon the faults of others or upon our environmental circumstances.

The reality, however, is that the fallen human heart is "deceitful above all things and desperately wicked; who can know it?" (Jeremiah 17:9). Fallen people are chronically resistant to the revelation of sin and human depravity, and as long as they resist this revelation they will persist in the hardness of their hearts and cut themselves off from the strong hand of love.

No one can possibly know the full condition of their own heart unless God reveals it to them. "Who can know it?" wrote Jeremiah. There is indeed something that people unaided by revelation simply cannot put their finger on; it is that elusive factor that many people simply never come to terms with. It is obvious that Freud, in his personal rejection of the Bible was, like so many others, trying to side-step the whole issue of sin. As we have already noted, the concept of sin is deeply abhorrent to secular psychotherapists because of the association of guilt and shame attached to the idea of "sin." Since guilt and shame are antithetical to a healthy self image, secular psychotherapists steer away from any concept that would promote these feelings.

The Heart and Natural Revelation

This entire discussion raises a very interesting point. Theologians draw out the distinction between what they call *natural* revelation and *special* revelation, which are two terms used in relation to our knowledge of God. Natural revelation refers to that which may be deductively known of God from observing the natural world; Paul discussed this theme in the first chapter of Romans. Special revelation, on the other hand, refers to that which God has specifically revealed to humanity through the divinely inspired Scriptures. We may infer from nature that there is a God who created the heavens and the earth, but we will forever be a bit fuzzy on the finer details of who this God is and what He is like.

This same principle applies to our understanding of human beings and their actual heart condition. We may infer certain things purely from observing human behavior but we may never understand the finer details. Sigmund Freud did his best, unaided by special revelation, to make certain observations about human behavior. He inferred that there were certain unconscious factors at work within us that motivate us to behave in certain ways, which are inconsistent with our conscious thought processes. He proposed that if we can only make some significant modifications to the way we think at an unconscious level, all our personal problems would be solved!

Because Freud rejected special revelation as it touched upon human nature, he was left to grope in the dark like the legend of the blind men and the elephant. According to this Indian tale, there were a number of blind men who had an encounter with an elephant and were asked to describe what they thought it was. One man felt the tail and thought it was a dangling rope. Another man felt the elephant's trunk and thought it was a giant water hose. Another blind man felt a leg and thought it was a tree trunk. Each of them had only part of the picture and could not comprehend the whole. Secular psychology has consistently fallen into this same error.

The best observations of fallen human nature, unaided by divine revelation, will at best give us a foggy explanation of the human condition and how we might remedy the problem. Left to our own reasoning capacities, we will always get it wrong. Fortunately, God has not left us to our own reasoning to come to an understanding of the fundamental problem with the human race. The Bible contains the only true "psychology" that is worthy of the term. Psychology, by definition, is the study of the human soul, and God has given us more understanding on the condition of the soul than we could ever digest in our lifetime.

As Christians, when we become entangled in un-biblical psychological speculations about the unconscious mind, we miss the point entirely. The starting point in developing a thoroughly biblical anthropology must always be the revelation of Scripture. From a biblical standpoint, it needs to be stated dogmatically that according to Scripture, fallen human nature does not consist of a conscious and an unconscious mind. Instead, Scripture confirms that fallen human beings have *a conscious mind and a sinful heart* that cannot be known or understood until the light of God penetrates the inner recesses of the heart.

It is evident that people's conscious thoughts and the actual condition of their heart are often in significant tension with each other. Someone may approve or disapprove of a certain expression of human behavior on a purely intellectual level, but it is the hidden purposes and motives of the heart that ultimately dictate and govern people's actions, whether they are aware of them or not. And because of the presence of sin in the fallen human heart, people seem relentlessly inclined toward selfish choices, even when these choices violate their noblest ideals.

When I studied theology at university, one of my lecturers used the analogy of the ball that is used in lawn bowling to describe the fallen human orientation toward sin. In lawn bowls, the ball has a "bias" produced by a lead weight in one side of the ball. No matter how straight you might try to bowl that ball, whenever it slows down it deviates to the side that the weight is in. Intellectually, people may agree with the truth of God's Word in its standard of righteousness and holiness, but something within their heart continually inclines them toward wickedness.

The obvious tension between people's conscious rationalizations and the mysterious inclinations of their own hearts has given rise to a plethora of fanciful speculations and theories by secular psychologists. It is not as though there is one standard model of human personality. The vast range of conflicting theories of human personality serves to highlight the urgent need for those in the pastoral, counselling, and healing ministries to re-focus upon the fundamental issue: the heart is unknowable apart from divine revelation. To the extent that people have lost touch with divine revelation, to that same extent they have lost touch with the revelatory knowledge of the heart.

One of the major themes of this series of books is to seek to refocus upon the centrality of divine revelation in the supernatural transformation of the heart. But before we get to this exciting revelation, we need to prepare the way. Part of this process now consists in the dismantling of ideas and concepts that have infiltrated the church. These ideas impede the development of a supernatural model of transformation that descends exclusively from above. The next chapter will hopefully be helpful for those of us who have found ourselves swept up in the rising tide of Christian integrationism.

Chapter Ten

The Biblical Versus Psycho-therapeutic Paradigm

Anna decided that the Lord was calling her to the counselling ministry. It was something that had been tugging on her heart for many years so she finally decided to enrol in a degree program in counselling that was on offer from one of the theological colleges in her city. She had been involved in counselling within her church but now she knew she needed credentialing. But six months into her course, she began to feel increasingly uncomfortable with the level of psychological material that she was obligated to read. The endless theories of human personality seemed to be taking her further and further away from the biblical material that she had always enjoyed reading before she commenced her degree.

At the end of the first year, she dropped out of the course because she realized she was being inundated with secular theories and drifting away from the straightforward principles of ministry that she practiced as part of her ministry team at church. She had seen the Lord supernaturally break through in people's lives so many times that she found the endless theories beginning to undermine her confidence in the sufficiency of Christ to set the captives free. She never ended up obtaining her degree, but she now enjoys a powerful ministry in which she sees the Lord bring significant breakthroughs through the power of the Holy Spirit in the lives of the people she ministers to.

We are living in a day in which the evangelical and Pentecostal/charismatic churches have been inundated by an avalanche of psychological theories and therapies. Tragically, very few believers feel the need to question or challenge the validity of integrating Christianity with these secular psychotherapies.

The theological havoc that this inundation has unleashed has been the focus of a growing number of Christian authors who have sought to evaluate the impact of integrationism upon Christianity. Integrationism is the technical term used to describe the present day integration of Christianity and secular psychotherapy.

As we saw in the previous chapter, psychologists tread on dangerous ground when they seek to define the human personality by proposing theories of personality that contradict biblical concepts. This is especially true when Christian counsellors weave these secular theories of the human personality into their counselling practice. The main area of concern for those of us who are concerned with biblical integrity comes from the practical arm of psychology, which is called "psychotherapy." As its name suggests, it is a therapeutic approach to healing the soul, and it is specifically within this field that this discipline begins to have a detrimental impact upon the outcome of Christian ministry. Some may beg to differ, but I would question to what extent they have received a revelation of the radical *heaven to earth model* of kingdom ministry that Jesus introduced. His ministry is completely supernatural from start to finish.

The crucial issue at stake in this ongoing debate is the contrast between *natural* techniques of human transformation with *supernatural* techniques of transformation. The transformational model introduced by Jesus was comprehensively supernatural from start to finish. His ministry was purely from above! Jesus' ministry begins with a person being born *from above*, and it unfolds through the supernatural intervention of the revelation, power, and love of God. God supernaturally demolishes every stronghold that would hinder a born again believer from entering into the fullness of the supernatural transformation promised to His redeemed sons and daughters. In fact, the biblical worldview radically critiques the subtle infiltration of naturalistic techniques into the arena of the supernatural ministry of transforming the human heart. This is foundational to the biblical framework.

For the purpose of clarification, whenever I speak negatively or disparagingly of either psychology or psychotherapy, I am speaking specifically of those concepts that violate a biblical understanding of people, specifically through the use of language and categories that are clearly at odds with biblical theology. So this would include all psychological theories of the human personality that shift the focus away from clear biblical categories. It would also include any form of counselling or therapy that springs forth from the integration of these secular theories with biblical counselling. My greatest concern with secular models of transformation is that they comprehensively fail to come to terms with new creation realities and implications of the miracle of spiritual regeneration. The centre of gravity for secular theories of personal change is naturalism, whereas the centre of gravity for the biblical model of transformation is supernaturalism.

Throughout this chapter, I am critiquing certain ideas and concepts; I am not criticizing people. In critiquing secular psychotherapy and Christian integrationism, I want to affirm the efforts of anyone in the pastoral or counselling profession who has invested their life into helping people overcome personal problems of living. The world is sinking fast in a quagmire of addiction, narcissism, depression, and deep sexual brokenness. Mental illnesses are continually on the rise and countless numbers of people desperately need some kind of help.

If you are reading this book and you work in this field, I applaud your compassion and your desire to help people to live in freedom from their brokenness. I am approaching this topic theologically and my primary concern is the *good* standing in the way of the *best*. In light of the escalating statistics in every arena of human brokenness, we urgently need to recover God's absolute best in the field of counselling and heart focused ministry. There are profound reasons for the biblical admonition to "examine everything carefully; [and to] hold fast to that which is good" (1 Thessalonians 5:21 NASB). So, with that admonition, let's proceed to explore the foundations of the Christian integrationist movement.

The Ascent of Christian Integrationism

If we trace the genesis of the integrationist movement and the context out of which it emerged, it helps considerably to shed light on the naturalistic origins of this approach to personal transformation. In a fascinating essay titled "Integration or Inundation?" David Powlison documents the gradual infiltration of psychology into the field of Christian counselling over the past sixty years. He points out that "before the 1950s only theological and ecclesiastical liberals embraced the psychologies and psychotherapies."[25] Christian psychologists gradually gained visibility and respectability within evangelicalism, initially through seminaries and colleges, because conservative evangelicals were consciously ill equipped to offer solutions to the personal and interpersonal problems that many Christians faced. Powlison observed, "Evangelicals lacked both intellectual and institutional resources to address people's problems in living."[26]

Into the vacuum stepped the professional Christian psychologists, arguing that the integration of the two disciplines was a legitimate pursuit because both sought the same ends: the wholeness of the individual. Once the concept of "integration" became accepted within theologically conservative colleges and seminaries, the avalanche began. Many institutions set up psychology faculties to better equip pastors to counsel their flocks, whilst the leading prophets of integrationism gained increased respectability within the church. Powlison observed:

Through books, articles, seminars, videotapes and radio broadcasts they became the evangelical authorities for solving problems in living. The evangelical psychotherapy community built its scholarly, institutional and popular base during the 1970s and 1980s.[27] In the late 1990s the inundation of psychology reached saturation point. This saturation of the therapeutic in evangelicalism reflected the growth of psychotherapy in modern western society.

Ideas that were once the province of professionals now inundated popular Christian literature. Most significantly, psychological categories increasingly became the language of daily life in evangelical circles. Words such as *self-esteem, dysfunctional family, codependency, needs, etc.,* suddenly seemed to capture the most significant things about life and God and the Bible. The best selling self-help books in Christian bookstores are psychologically flavoured (e.g. David Seamands, Larry Crabb, Minirth and Meier). A colleague recently told me of his conversation with the manager of a large Christian bookstore. He asked, "What's hot these days?" The man replied, "Anything with 'pain' in the title. I can't keep the shelves stocked because they sell so fast!"[28]

What began as an attempt to supplement an apparent weakness within the evangelical churches has slowly reached epidemic proportions. No one could deny that from a theological perspective there are some pressing questions that need to be asked about the presuppositional underpinnings of the integrationist movement. The most important issue that integrationism raises is the question of what the sixteenth century Reformers called the principle of *Sola Scriptura*. During the Reformation, the burning theological issue was the relationship between tradition, Scripture, and authority. From a biblical perspective, Martin Luther enunciated the principle of *Sola Scriptura* to demonstrate that the Scriptures alone were the basis of authority in the Christian's life and that human tradition must always be subordinate to Scripture.

The primary issue that integrationism raises is whether the Scriptures sanction the supplementation of the biblical concept of "counsel" with anything that has its origin in human wisdom. From a biblical perspective, there is a wisdom from above that is deliberately contrasted with a wisdom that is "earthly" (James 3:15). "But the wisdom that is from above is first pure" (James 3:17). This is a pure heavenly wisdom that proceeds from the heart and mind of God. It is pure because it hasn't been contaminated by anything from earth. Integrationism is the merging of a secular discipline with Christian ideas that exist independently of biblical theology. The foundational argument against the philosophy of integrationism is that the biblical worldview expressed in the pages of Scripture strictly forbids the mixture of any secular ideas with biblical revelation. This is a theme that runs all the way through the Bible. If a vacuum existed in the 1950s in which Bible-believing Christians felt they were unable to effectively counsel people who had deep problems in living, then rather than embracing the wisdom of this present age, why not search the Scriptures and seek the Lord for a greater spiritual equipping to meet the needs of the day?

It is interesting to reflect upon the state of mind that led to the idea that the solution to man's problems could not be found in the Word of God and the power of the Holy Spirit. How would Jesus respond to the suggestion that the church needed help from secular psychologists to successfully transform the human heart? If Jesus came to the earth in the twenty-first century, would He have succumbed to the pressure to integrate His message with the "wisdom" of the secular psycho-therapeutic community?

The glaring theological implications of such a suggestion highlights a significant deficit of biblical revelation in the church. We could also ask what this says about a person's revelation of the majesty and supernatural power of Jesus Christ. While it may not come as a great shock for theological liberals to embrace the trends of *secularization* within the church, it is yet another thing to come to terms with evangelicals embracing a secular discipline when evangelicalism itself was founded upon the principle of *Sola Scriptura*. Consider the irony of the situation: today we have evangelicals who have forsaken the rallying cry of their own founding fathers by renouncing the bedrock principle upon which their own reformation movement was founded.

Those who look away from Christ to seek the assistance of natural human techniques and therapies can only do so when their vision of the person of Christ and the power of the cross has been significantly compromised. God has no questions about His ability to meet every single human need, no matter how great it is or how seemingly impossible it appears to be from our human perspective. "Behold, I am the Lord, the God of all flesh. *Is there anything too hard for Me?*" (Jeremiah 32:27). Jesus was continually faced with the unbelief of His disciples who were overwhelmed by seemingly impossible problems. "But Jesus looked at them and said to them, '... *with God all things are possible*'" (Matthew 19:26).

God has committed the wealth of His unlimited resources to the complete restoration and transformation of His people. "He who did not spare His own Son, but delivered Him up for us all, how shall He not with Him also freely give us *all things*" (Romans 8:32)? "His divine power has given to us *all things* that pertain to life and godliness, through the knowledge of Him who called us by glory and virtue" (2 Peter 1:3). The subtle secularization of the church exposes a glaring deficit in our revelatory knowledge of God.

Ultimately, any drift toward the secularization of Christianity represents a subtle apostasy from the God of the Bible. The vacuum that led to the integration of Christianity and secular thought was not merely an intellectual vacuum but *a loss of faith in the power of God.* This has historically been called *liberalism*, the essence of which has been to strip the Bible of its supernatural element and to undermine the confidence of Christians in the raw supernatural power of God.

Powlison's observation that prior to the 1950s only liberals were attracted to psychology, is particularly relevant in this context.

If the church of the past sixty years had been gripped with a vision of the all-powerful God, would the folly of human wisdom have held any attraction whatsoever? Some people may take exception to the thought that the insights of the secular psychologists are mere human wisdom. Advocates of integrationism often argue that "all truth is God's truth," and that God is therefore the author of the transformational insights of psychology. The question that needs to be answered by those who raise this contention is: can we in any way add to the wisdom of the power of the cross? Is the cross at the centre of every integrationist model of ministry? Definitely not! We can say confidently that it represents a subtle secularization of the church if a particular model of ministry deviates from the centrality of the new creation miracle and the power of the cross.

God's answer to the plight of humanity is not great therapies and naturalistic techniques but the power of the cross. Jesus had no interest in putting a new patch on an old garment. "No one puts a piece from a new garment on an old one; otherwise the new makes a tear, and also the piece that was taken out of the new does not match the old. And no one puts new wine into old wineskins; or else the new wine will burst the wineskins and be spilled, and the wineskins will be ruined. But new wine must be put into new wineskins, and both are preserved" (Luke 5:36-38). The message of the Bible is that there is no hope for the old garment. It must be replaced with a completely new garment.

The "old man" cannot be rehabilitated. He must be put to death in order to release the glory of the "new man." The gospel of the cross is the wisdom of God but this wisdom is hidden from the wise and prudent of this age. "Jesus rejoiced in the Spirit and said, "I thank You, Father, Lord of heaven and earth, that You have hidden these things from the wise and prudent and revealed them to babes. Even so, Father, for so it seemed good in Your sight" (Luke 10:21). If a Christian invests his or her time and energy into a therapeutic technique to try to "re-program the unconscious mind," we must ask the question if he or she has had a revelation of the transformational power of the cross!

In the past, times of great revival have prompted God's people to cast off their compromise with the world, whether they embraced "Asherah poles" or secular philosophies. Today, the psychological seduction of Christianity is merely a symptom of a far deeper malady: a lack of familiarity with the God of the Bible and a lack of revelation of the supernatural power of the cross. It is far more consistent with the biblical worldview to say that secular psychology filled a vacuum that existed in the late twentieth century because the church had not been in a state of revival. If we do not have the power of God to deliver the captives from their prison, whatever their bondage may be, do we turn to the arm of the flesh to supplement our lack of power or do we begin to cry out for a mighty outpouring of the power of God to equip us to destroy the works of the evil one and to set the captives free? Our response to this question will depend upon whom we are taking our counsel from.

As we reflect upon the condition of the church over the past sixty years and the mess we are in today as a result of the choices of our spiritual forefathers, we can safely say that the church's fling with psychology has been a serious mistake. Seen in its broadest sociological context our current demise is the fruit of our *cultural captivity*. Os Guinness, in a fascinating essay titled "America's Last Men and their Magnificent Talking Cure," discusses the surrender of evangelicalism over the past generation, to what he calls the "therapeutic revolution." The therapeutic revolution is a term coined by sociologists to describe the profound transformation that modern society has undergone since the ascent of Freud and his disciples. The influence of this revolution is so pervasive that sociologists speak of modern Western culture as the psychological society. Os Guinness writes:

> Where the American church at large and the evangelical community in particular have been unguarded about the therapeutic, they have been caught in the toils of a new Babylonian captivity. But this captivity is enforced on couches instead of brick-kilns and experienced in affinity groups instead of chain gangs.[29]

Recognizing that the therapeutic revolution, as a social phenomenon, has touched every fibre of modern life helps to explain why it has been so difficult for the church, in its un-revived state, to resist being swept along with the tide of this social movement. Guinness continues:

> The triumph of the therapeutic has finally transformed psychology from a mere discipline to a world-view and a way of life. Triumphing as a social revolution, the therapeutic has gained a self-evident status and a taken-for-granted cultural authority that is rarely questioned.... Psychology has woven itself into the warp and woof of everyday life and speech. From such early terms as "unconscious" to such recent ones as "codependency," the jargon of psychology has become the coin of everyday life.[30]

The Magnificent "Talking Cure"

As with many popular social trends, the church has capitulated to the inexorable pressure to conform to the world. But what has been so remarkable about this capitulation is the enthusiasm with which the church has made the transition. As Os Guinness points out:

> What is overlooked in this enthusiasm is the oddness of the liaison between the gospel and the therapeutic movement.

Freud offered the benefits of psychology as a human "talking cure." Surely this is a curious remedy for those committed to the objective and supernatural work of divine healing![31]

Guinness was likely alluding to Paul's famous adage, "For the kingdom of God is not a matter of *talk* but of *power!*" (1 Corinthians 4:20). In the final analysis, the Christian cannot bring anyone to a condition of wholeness through mere talk. Talk will always play an important role in Christian counselling but our "talk," in contrast with the talk of secular therapists, always points to an encounter with a supernatural, all-powerful God who seeks to pour out His power upon broken people to set the captives free. Any "Christian" model of personal transformation where talk is the exclusive focus represents what Paul called a "form of godliness that denies its power" (2 Timothy 3:5). The church is the sole steward of the dynamic power of God that transforms the human heart. We dare not sell our birthright as Esau did for a morsel of food (Hebrews 12:16).

Wholeness for the Christian comes through a life changing power encounter with this all-powerful God. So unless our model of ministry and counselling has as its centerpiece the supernatural power of God to transform the human heart, we are succumbing to a technique of counselling that resembles the secular therapist, rather than the supernatural ministry of Christ. Talking always plays a role in ministering to those who are broken and bruised, but true kingdom-based counselling must always be seen as an expression of the kingdom ministry of Christ. Only Christ has broken into this present evil age with the "powers of the age to come" (Hebrews 6:5) in order to destroy the works of the devil.

In the kingdom of God, the supreme focus of the Christian is on the Lord Jesus Christ who rose from the dead through the supernatural power of God, declaring, "All power has been given to Me in heaven and on earth" (Matthew 28:18). The fact that the power of Christ is freely available to transform everyone who believes is why

Paul warned the disciples of the Lord, "Beware lest anyone cheat you through philosophy and empty deceit, according to the tradition of men, according to the basic principles of the world, and not according to Christ" (Colossians 2:8).

Jesus Christ is the power of God! He was clothed in the Spirit of counsel and of power. "The Spirit of the Lord will rest on Him; the Spirit of wisdom and of understanding, ***the Spirit of counsel and of power***, the Spirit of knowledge and of the fear of the Lord" (Isaiah 11:2 NIV). Talk was never intended to be divorced from supernatural power. Whenever Paul spoke, he always talked about God's power as the key to human transformation. "For our gospel did not come to you in word only, but also in power, and in the Holy Spirit" (1 Thessalonians 1:5). To Paul's mind, an empty philosophy was one that was devoid of supernatural power!

As a Roman citizen living in the midst of the ascendency of Greek philosophy, Paul was overwhelmingly conscious of the conflict between two sources of power: the enticing power of human wisdom to solve humanity's problems and the life-changing power of God. In this vein he said, "My speech and my preaching were not with persuasive words of human wisdom, but in demonstration of the Spirit and of power, that your faith should not be in the wisdom of men but in the power of God" (1 Corinthians 2:4-5). Because the powers of the age to come have broken in through the person of Christ, our faith is to rest solely on Him. Jim Owen, in his provocative book, *Christian Psychology's War on God's Word*, says,

> No matter how unintentional it may be, the evangelical community is being taught not to look to the Word of God for understanding and solving its problems, not to experience the reality of God's power promised to us in Christ and by Christ, but, rather, to depend upon the word of the psychologist to live a victorious Christian life. Christ said, "My grace is sufficient." "Christian" psychology says: "not without my assistance."[32]

Enter, the Power of the Spirit

The evangelical church has undergone a powerful transformation in the past sixty years. By and large, back in the days when the evangelicals first began to embrace secular psychology, the movement was largely non-charismatic in its theology and experience. The evangelicalism of the 1950s and 1960s was almost completely under the spell of cessationist theology with its bold assertion that the gifts of the Holy Spirit ceased at the close of the apostolic age. The integrationist movement is a product of this era of non-charismatic Christianity. Since that time, a significant portion of the evangelical church has been powerfully impacted by two significant waves of the power of the Holy Spirit.

The first wave of the Spirit's power came in the Pentecostal revival of the first decade of the twentieth century; this movement gave birth to Pentecostalism, which needs to be differentiated from its more scholarly cousin called evangelicalism. The second wave came in the charismatic renewal of the 1960s, which impacted many mainstream evangelical denominations. The next wave has been called the "third wave" movement by Dr. C. Peter Wagner. This third wave of renewal gave birth to entire new movements and denominations that were characterized by gift-based ministry. One of the most notable movements to emerge out of this third wave of renewal in the church was the Vineyard Movement under the leadership of John Wimber.

Two third wave theologians, Gary S. Greig and Kevin N. Springer, outline the significance of this new move of the Holy Spirit within evangelicalism in their book, *The Kingdom and the Power*.

> The third wave, Wagner says, is analogous to the first two waves of the Holy Spirit's work in the Pentecostal and Charismatic movements. However, third wave proponents distinguish their theology and practice from that of Pentecostals and Charismatics in certain ways. Although third wave proponents are open to all the miraculous gifts

and miraculous work of God they generally understand the baptism of the Spirit not as a second blessing but as part of conversion. At the same time, the third wave acknowledges the need to be filled and empowered by the Holy Spirit more than once after conversion. They emphasise the potential of all Christians, not just specially gifted persons, to minister healing and to minister with all the miraculous gifts.

Third wave proponents claim that the renewal has brought several positive elements to evangelicalism, including a greater understanding and openness to the work and power of the Holy Spirit taught in Scripture. They have begun to move from an unbalanced emphasis based only on the proclaimed Word to a scripturally balanced emphasis on both the proclaimed Word and ministry in God's power. Proponents of third wave theology and practice claim to have attempted such a biblical balance – a balance between the fruit of the Spirit and the gifts of the Spirit, between the proclamation of the gospel and the works of healing and gift-based ministry, which are said to demonstrate the power of Christ in the gospel.[33]

In this third significant outpouring of the Holy Spirit that began in the late twentieth century, previously non-charismatic and even anti-charismatic evangelicals have been powerfully impacted by the Holy Spirit. They have had their entire understanding of Christianity turned upside down. For the first time in the history of evangelicalism, the charismatic wing of the evangelical movement has become the majority. This milestone was reached in the first decade of the new millennium when fifty-one percent of evangelicals identified themselves as charismatic. Those evangelicals who have been impacted personally by this outpouring of the Spirit have begun to combine the strengths of evangelicalism with its strong foundation of biblical scholarship and the power of the Holy Spirit.

The Biblical Versus Psycho-therapeutic Paradigm

Many third wave proponents call themselves *Empowered Evangelicals*. As the third wave movement has matured, it has given rise to some excellent theology that represents a new apostolic paradigm. This paradigm is centred in the power of the Holy Spirit and gift-based ministry. Springer and Greig note that "the term 'gift-based ministry' refers to ministry with all spiritual gifts, including the miraculous gifts that, as Scriptural examples from the Gospels, Acts, and the Epistles show, demonstrate God's presence and power in a dramatic way (prophecy, word of knowledge, word of wisdom, gifts of healing, working of miracles, distinguishing spirits, tongues, interpretation)."[34] This historic shift within evangelicalism has literally revolutionized the understanding of Christian ministry and has led to a number of significant reforms in ministry practice.

The question that now needs to be asked is: what place does integrationism have in this new theological paradigm? I would like to suggest that a new reformation is needed in the arena of Christian ministry and counselling. This field of study needs to be brought up to speed with the transformation that evangelicalism has undergone in the past few decades. Charismatic evangelicals are now the majority within the evangelical movement and the percentage of evangelicals who are abandoning non-charismatic evangelicalism steadily increases. Integrationism is an old ministry wineskin that was a legacy of a traditional evangelicalism. This evangelicalism was often under the spell of a cessationist theology. If we are to keep in step with the Holy Spirit as He leads the church into all truth, we must dispense with old models of ministry that have been proven redundant or not Scripturally based.

As a reflection of traditional evangelicalism, the old ministry wineskin of integrationism had its focus *exclusively* on words: the great "talking cure" as Os Guinness described it. Under the new wineskin, the paradigm has shifted to the marriage of the Word and the power of the Spirit. It has not dispensed with the talk aspect of Christian ministry because the gospel is always communicated through the medium of words. Rather, the new paradigm represents a return to the apostolic and prophetic ministry of the first century. There will always be cessationist evangelicals who pride themselves in being "word only" people. But Paul explicitly warned against this dangerous trend. "For our gospel did not come to you in ***word only***, but also in power, and in the Holy Spirit and in much assurance" (1 Thessalonians 1:5). The power of God is freely available to demolish strongholds that can never be overcome by mere words.

The re-emergence of prophetic ministry, for example, has tremendous implications for the ministry of counselling. Under the old paradigm, God knows the hearts of men but has only revealed the nature of the human heart in broad-brush strokes in the Scriptures. Non-charismatics who sought to minister to people's hearts had to do so exclusively from the Scriptures. What good is it if God knows our hearts but does not speak to His people personally or directly, as the non-charismatic evangelicals assert? Under the new theological paradigm, God has an intimate knowledge of the heart of every single man, woman, and child, and He speaks through the gift of prophecy and words of knowledge directly into the ministry situation. This model of ministry is entirely consistent with Apostolic Christianity.

Paul indicated that one of the functions of the gift of prophecy was that through the ministry of the prophetic, the secrets of the human heart were revealed (1 Corinthians 14:24-25). A prophetically gifted minister may receive a piece of prophetic information directly from God in the form of a vision, a picture, or a word of knowledge. This information can unlock the ministry time, resulting in tremendous freedom. I have seen this time and time again in our own local church ministry. The development of the prophetic has comprehensively revolutionized our ministry model, such that we now rely exclusively upon God to break through in the ministry time to unlock the human heart.

This reality alone is revolutionizing Christian ministry and restoring apostolic power back to centre stage. Apostolic power releases apostolic fruitfulness, and the fruit of this kind of ministry is evidenced in the quantum transformation that many parts of the church are currently experiencing. The restoration of power ministries in the church represents as significant a transformation as the theological reformation of the sixteenth century. Gift-based ministry brings God back into each unique ministry situation, because Jesus Himself walks into the room and ministers powerfully to the hearts and minds of those seeking freedom. The theological implications of this transformation are still being processed as theologians and church historians wrestle with the changes that this new gift-based ministry paradigm represents. C. Peter Wagner is calling this new expression of the church the "New Apostolic Reformation," arguing that the dynamic changes occurring throughout the church in the twenty-first century represent a restoration of authentic apostolic ministry.

Within the context of this new reformation, it is only a matter of time until the old paradigm of integrationism collapses under its own weight. The church's love affair with psychotherapy is doomed to recede into history in the light of the glory of the emerging ministry paradigm. The Holy Spirit is restoring the kingdom ministry of Jesus to centre stage, and this restoration is making the old paradigm appear more and more as an anachronism from a by-gone age. God is restoring an apostolic knowledge of the heart to the church and an apostolic model of ministry to meet the deepest needs of those who are languishing under the weight of sin and brokenness.

The wisdom of the psycho-therapeutic "talking cure" pales in comparison to the unveiling of the glorious ministry of Jesus Christ. It is not just the secular and Christian psycho-therapeutic communities that are enamoured by the promise of the great talking cure. Even non-integrationist evangelicals have fallen into the trap of reducing Christianity to a mere "talking cure" that is often devoid of the power of the Spirit to bring transformation. The theological orthodoxy of evangelicalism can minister death instead of life when it is reduced to mere talk and divorced from the power of God. Even in his own day, Paul was deeply concerned that Christianity would be reduced to a religion that denied the power that was inherent to its supernatural origins (2 Timothy 3:5). That is why he proclaimed that the kingdom of God was not a matter of mere talk but of supernatural power.

Integrationism and Modernist Captivity

Seen in its broadest context, the phenomenon of integrationism is one of the defining characteristics of the church's captivity to modernism. The process of liberating the church from its captivity to modernism is still largely unfinished. The Holy Spirit is working in the hearts and minds of Western believers to extricate them from the shackles of the modernist mind-set. This humanistic mind-set that rose to prominence in the period of the Enlightenment in the seventeenth century had a strong anti-supernatural bias. The emerging philosophy of naturalism gradually undermined the supernatural presuppositions of the pre-modern era, culminating in the emergence of Darwinian evolution. The exaltation of human reason over divine revelation eventually gave rise to the phenomenon of theological liberalism. This liberalism rejected the concept of the divine inspiration of Scripture and a belief in the miraculous.

Anti-charismatic and non-charismatic evangelicalism was also the direct result of the church's capitulation to modernism, with its overt anti-supernaturalism. Even those who adhered to the concept of divine inspiration found themselves bowing down to the power of human reason under the intimidation of the exultant claims of rationalism. The power of the mind gradually became the centre of gravity for evangelicals, rather than the power of the Holy Spirit. Evangelical scholarship replaced the anointing of the Holy Spirit. The marriage of Christianity and secular psychotherapy was conducted under the mistletoe of rationalism with its arrogant exaltation of human reason over divine revelation. The whole integrationist movement is a manifestation of the church's cultural captivity to modernism and rationalism. It is an old ministry wineskin that cannot contain the new wine of the Holy Spirit.

But the status quo is beginning to change. We are in the early stages of the apostolic reformation. This restoration process will have enormous ramifications for the church as God restores everything that has been lost through its capitulation to modernism. An apostolic knowledge of the heart combined with apostolic power to minister to the heart will relegate the folly of integrationism to its rightful place in church history. The apostolic reformation has been preceded by decades of prayer for the church to be restored. God is answering this global prayer movement with an unprecedented revelation of the glory of Jesus Christ and His power to transform people's lives. It is this revelation of Christ and His "incomparably great power for us who believe" that is shifting the centre of gravity away from human reason and back to the power of the Holy Spirit.

My purpose in deconstructing the presuppositional underpinnings of the Christian integrationist movement is merely to clear the way for a much greater revelation of Christ and His power to change people's lives. Ishmael came before Isaac, but Isaac was the child of promise. It seems that the long-awaited appearance of the true promises of God are oftentimes preceded by Ishmael styled ministries. People frequently become satisfied with what they presently have but this often stands in the way of the new thing that God is seeking to establish through His Spirit. Integrationism is a case of the good standing in the way of the best. I have been to the top of the mountain and have seen something that is so much greater than what we currently have in the western church.

Integrationists are well-intentioned ministers of Christ, and their passion to implement their psycho-therapeutic techniques for the betterment of humanity is to be applauded. But when a particular ministry model stands in the way of something even greater being revealed, then it becomes a theological issue that needs to be addressed. My vision for the restoration of the glorious prophetic ministry of Christ to the heart compels me to deconstruct a philosophy of ministry that has become an impediment to the full restoration of the kingdom ministry of Jesus. We are discussing two starkly contrasting models of ministry, and the purpose of this chapter is to juxtapose the integrationist model and the kingdom model of ministry.

I have friends who are integrationists and their ministry has clearly been beneficial to broken people. Psychologists have done an excellent job in identifying a broad spectrum of psychological disorders. These disorders are very real and they frequently cripple people from functioning properly. My contention is not with the diagnosis of these disorders, but with the application of therapeutic techniques that are founded on the power of human reason to overcome what are essentially spiritual problems. We are living in a highly psychologized society where people are more aware of the existence of psychological disorders than ever before. But without the kingdom ministry of Jesus, people lack the supernatural power of the Holy Spirit and the unconditional love of the Father that is essential to overcome their personal problems.

Not all evangelicals resonate with the integrationist movement. Some evangelicals have reacted so violently to the integrationist movement that they have taken up a personal campaign against any Christian ministry that in any way compromises with the insights of secular psychotherapy. I refuse to be identified with this witch-hunt approach. I consider myself to be a non-integrationist rather than a militant anti-integrationist, and there is a significant difference. There are many insights that we may receive from Christian authors and teachers who are committed integrationists without embracing the integrationist presuppositions that undergird their model of ministry.

The Biblical Versus Psycho-therapeutic Paradigm

Just because someone is an integrationist does not mean that God does not give him or her significant insights into the human heart. Most authors in the field of biblical counselling have valuable contributions to make to our knowledge of the heart, irrespective of their position in the integrationist debate. Their depth of counselling experience has placed them in a position where God has given them some profound insights into the human heart, even though they might interpret their insights through an integrationist paradigm, sometimes even using integrationist language.

David Powlison differentiates between what he calls "thoughtful integrationists" and "careless integrationists." He says, "Thoughtful integrationists filter out a lot more than careless integrationists. But no integrationist sees the complete paradigm shift that the sufficient Scripture offers."[35] Powlison notes that as a rule, "Integrationists do not provide vigorous and perceptive biblical categories both for explaining people and for stemming the psychologizing tide. The centre of gravity and interest for even the most careful and theologically astute integrationists is psychology. The centre of gravity for effective counselling and de-psychologizing the evangelical church must be Scripture."[36]

Without a comprehensive knowledge of the Scriptures and an understanding of the building blocks of biblical theology, it becomes difficult to differentiate between insights that are solidly anchored in Scripture and those insights that are based in secular psychological theories. We can only do this effectively if we know the Scriptures well. Jesus promised that the Holy Spirit would lead us into all truth (John 16:13). He will also lead us out of ideas and concepts that are not from above. As I have sought to grow in the revelatory knowledge of the heart, I have been challenged by the Lord to only use biblical language in the development of my understanding of the human heart.

As we draw out all the truths of the Scriptures on a given theme, we can build them together into the development of a systematic theology. I am convinced that a systematic theology of the heart can be developed from the biblical material that does not violate the integrity of the Scriptures by importing ideas and concepts that are foreign to the biblical writers. It is one of the goals of biblical hermeneutics to allow the authors of the Scriptures to speak out of their own historical context without imposing a contemporary understanding upon their writings.

Learning to Speak God's Language

Language is important to God because language is a code that conveys specific information. If we want to communicate effectively, we must be sure that those to whom we speak understand our language clearly, otherwise there will be a breakdown of communication. God speaks a particular language. The terms and concepts He uses to communicate are designed to convey highly specific concepts. The Christian faith requires precise language to communicate what are sometimes technical concepts. Throughout church history, Christians have appreciated the necessity of precision in the nomenclature that was used by the church.

To illustrate how seriously this was taken, we need look no further than the history of the creeds and councils of the early church. As the leaders of the fourth century church thrashed out the finer points of the doctrine of Christ and the Trinity, the adoption of certain highly specific technical words ultimately led to the split between East and West, which gave rise to the Eastern Orthodox tradition and the Western church headed by Rome. This historic split was over a single word: *homoousios*.[37] I am not suggesting that we become quite as pedantic, but we have been given a body of revelation from heaven that uses highly specific language.

The Biblical Versus Psycho-therapeutic Paradigm

Nowadays, we find all sorts of words used in the church, many of which are highly non-specific. Take "codependency" for example. It is hard to find any unanimity in defining this word, even in secular circles. "Dysfunctional" is another word that belongs to the domain of secular psychology that has slipped into popular usage within the church. What does it mean? Well, it all depends on how you define "functional" and that is where the debate begins. "Addiction" is another word that comes out of the recovery movement but is now commonly used to replace a number of technical biblical words. Instead of hearing a person's problem being described as "lust," it is common to hear this condition now described as a "sexual addiction." We are also told that our problem is not so much "sin" but a lack of "self-esteem." Instead of speaking about the "heart," it is now common to speak of the "unconscious mind." And so the list goes on.

All of this begs the question: if the church has spent hundreds of years fussing over the precise use of words to define theological concepts, why have we suddenly dispensed with the need for a technically precise language by readily embracing the language of Babylon? Has God suddenly dispensed with the need for technically correct language? Should we be worrying about the precision of our nomenclature when we are discussing human problems? The answer, of course, is yes! Christians are not called to use the language of the world, but to learn the pure language of God. If we are to communicate with God, we must learn the meaning of new theological words that describe spiritual realities. The Holy Spirit endorses the use of highly specific words, often passing by other words in order to describe spiritual realities. Paul said:

> For who among men knows the thoughts of a man except the man's spirit within him? In the same way no one knows the thoughts of God except the Spirit of God. We have not received the spirit of the world but the Spirit who is from God, that we may understand what God has freely given us. This

is what we speak, not in words taught us by human wisdom *but in words taught by the Spirit, expressing spiritual truths in spiritual words* (1 Corinthians 2:11-13 NIV).

A common nomenclature is the basis of true spiritual unity. Paul said, "Now I plead with you, brethren, by the name of our Lord Jesus Christ, that you all *speak the same thing*, and that there be no divisions among you, but that you be perfectly joined together in the same mind and in the same judgment" (1 Corinthians 1:10). The Lord Himself said through the prophet Zephaniah, "For then I will restore to the peoples *a **pure language*** that they all may call on the name of the Lord, to serve Him with one accord" (Zephaniah 3:9). Without a commonly agreed upon language, there can be no true unity.

What this means is that the intrusion of secular psycho-therapeutic terminology (or *psychobabble* as some have called it) into the church actually has profound implications for the Christian faith. What if some Christians adopt certain psychological terminology and some do not, could we all speak the same thing and be of the same mind and the same judgment? What if some Christians started using psychobabble in the language of hymns and worship songs? Would this be appropriate, and would everyone feel comfortable using this language in songs of worship?

There is a pure language that God has called us to speak, and that biblical language is the basis of our supernatural unity. The "*pure language*" endorsed by the prophet Zephaniah is a language that is not defiled by the impurity of the earth. It is a heavenly language that conveys powerful heavenly truths. What we are witnessing with the emergence of Christian integrationism is a confusion of languages, a new Babel within the church. If we would attune ourselves to the Holy Spirit, we will never hear Him speak with the nomenclature of the world. He has his own doctrinally precise terminology that we must take the time to learn if we would understand the things of the Spirit.

The Holy Spirit does not change His mind. The words He used in the inspiration of the Scriptures are the same words He uses today, words such as sin, sanctification, redemption, repentance, forgiveness, atonement, propitiation, deliverance, strongholds, holiness, and so on. The language of God is the language of the heart. God's eyes are ever upon the human heart, and His concerns centre on the issues of our heart. If we would commune with God, we must learn to speak His language. And if we would hear the voice of God, we must learn to understand the language of the Spirit. Let's get in step with the Spirit as He unveils the glorious kingdom ministry of Jesus to the heart.

Chapter Eleven

Becoming the Head and not the Tail

> If you listen to these commands of the Lord your God and carefully obey them, the Lord will make you the head and not the tail, and you will always have the upper hand.
> (Deuteronomy 28:13 NLT)

The extraordinary depth of Solomon's prophetic insight into the nature of the human heart became the Old Testament benchmark of prophetic wisdom. Solomon's name has become synonymous with wisdom. His unparalleled wisdom has had an ever-increasing sphere of influence. Saints in every generation have pondered the unique insights of the book of Proverbs. But in Solomon's own day his wisdom also had a profound impact, not only on the nation of Israel, but also on the surrounding nations, even as far away as North Africa. The book of Kings records the geographic impact of the prophetic insight that God gave Solomon.

> God gave Solomon wisdom and exceedingly great understanding, and largeness of heart as measureless as the sand on the seashore. Solomon's wisdom was greater than the wisdom of all the men of the East, and greater than all the wisdom of Egypt. He was wiser than any other man, and his fame

spread to all the surrounding nations. He spoke three thousand proverbs and his songs numbered a thousand and five. And men of all nations, from all the kings of the earth who had heard of his wisdom, came to hear the wisdom of Solomon (1 Kings 4:29-34).

One of those rulers who came to hear Solomon's wisdom was the Queen of Sheba. Even Jesus spoke of the time when this African Queen came to sit at Solomon's feet to listen to the great wisdom that the Lord had given him. Jesus said, "The queen of Sheba will rise up against this generation on judgment day and condemn it, because she came from a distant land to hear the wisdom of Solomon. And now someone greater than Solomon is here – and you refuse to listen to Him" (Matthew 12:42 NLT).

Solomon's wisdom was a gift from God. It was not something that he could claim any credit for. Jesus, on the other hand, claimed to be the very source of divine wisdom. His wisdom was not a gift from God, because in Christ "are hidden all the treasures of wisdom and knowledge" (Colossians 2:3). According to Paul, "Christ is the mighty power of God and the wonderful wisdom of God" (1 Corinthians 1:24 NLT). That is why Jesus could humbly claim to be "someone greater than Solomon."

Let's take a close look at the story of the Queen of Sheba visiting King Solomon, because it has a number of important insights into the strategic role of divine wisdom to impact the nations. There is no doubt that God poured out this unprecedented divine wisdom upon Solomon as a sign to the nations. Solomon's fame spread to all the surrounding nations so that "kings from every nation sent their ambassadors to listen to the wisdom of Solomon" (1 Kings 4:34).

> Now when the Queen of Sheba heard of the fame of Solomon, she came to Jerusalem to test Solomon with hard questions, having a very great caravan, camels that bore spices, gold

in abundance, and precious stones; and when she came to Solomon, she spoke with him about all that was in her heart. So Solomon answered all her questions; there was nothing so difficult for Solomon that he could not explain it to her. And when the Queen of Sheba had seen the wisdom of Solomon, the house that he had built, the food on his table, the seating of his servants, the service of his waiters and their apparel, his cupbearers and their apparel, and his entryway by which he went up to the house of the Lord, there was no more spirit in her. Then she said to the king: "It was a true report which I heard in my own land about your words and your wisdom. However I did not believe their words until I came and saw with my own eyes; and indeed the half of the greatness of your wisdom was not told me. You exceed the fame of which I heard. Happy are your men and happy are these your servants, who stand continually before you and hear your wisdom! Blessed be the Lord your God, who delighted in you, setting you on His throne to be king for the Lord your God! Because your God has loved Israel, to establish them forever, therefore He made you king over them, to do justice and righteousness." And she gave the king one hundred and twenty talents of gold, spices in great abundance, and precious stones; there never were any spices such as those the Queen of Sheba gave to King Solomon (2 Chronicles 9:1-9).

King Solomon was clearly an Old Testament type of Christ. His life prophetically foreshadowed the unveiling of Christ, whom we now acknowledge as the wisdom of God incarnate. Jesus said that He was even greater than Solomon because His wisdom radically transcended the wisdom of Solomon. If the Queen of Sheba was overwhelmed by Solomon's wisdom, just imagine how much more she would have been impressed by the wisdom of Jesus: the "greater than Solomon." Even at the age of twelve, Jesus astonished the religious teachers with His insight, understanding, and answers to their difficult questions.[38]

There are over fifty references in the gospel narratives to people being "astonished" or "marvelling" at the ministry of Jesus. Jesus answered questions about the human heart that people were not even asking! If anyone ever reached the point of asking a pertinent question about the human heart, they would discover that Jesus had already given the answer. Jesus spoke from the perspective of heaven concerning the fallen human condition, and His words unveiled the deepest secrets of the hidden person of the heart. He understood the heart of every person He ever met. He knew exactly what to say to minister to the deepest issues within every person whom He encountered.

Never in the history of humanity has there been someone with such profound insight into the human condition as Jesus. His depth of understanding of the human heart was entirely unparalleled. He exercised an x-ray vision into people's true heart condition so He knew whom He could trust and who He couldn't trust. John noted this uncanny quality of Jesus, citing an incident where Jesus perceived a situation that looked positive on the surface but He discerned the true condition of the people's hearts. "Now while He was in Jerusalem at the Passover Feast, many people saw the miraculous signs He was doing and believed in His name. But Jesus would not entrust Himself to them, for He knew all men. He did not need man's testimony about man, for He knew what was in man" (John 2:23-25 NIV). The *New Living Translation* of this verse says, "Many people were convinced that he was indeed the Messiah. But Jesus didn't trust them, because He knew what people were really like. No one needed to tell Him about human nature."

Throughout His ministry, Jesus continually displayed an unearthly supernatural wisdom. The people were "astonished at His teaching."[39] His reputation soon spread to the surrounding nations of Syria and beyond the Jordan.[40] His fame came to the attention of kings, rulers, and wise men from the East. On one occasion, "There were certain Greeks among those who came up to worship at the feast.

Then they came to Philip and asked him, saying, 'Sir, we wish to see Jesus'" (John 12:20-21). Paul tells us that the "Greeks seek after wisdom" (1 Corinthians 1:22). John intentionally called Jesus the *Logos* because the Logos, according to Greek philosophers, was the personification of divine wisdom.

The wisdom of Christ has impacted more people in history than any other single historical figure. His fame has spread abroad throughout all nations. His words are so profound that they have travelled to the ends of the earth. Like Solomon, Jesus also taught extensively on the heart of the wise and the heart of the fool. The people marvelled at His depth of insight saying, "Where did this Man get this wisdom?" (Matthew 13:54). And here is the point: this supernatural wisdom has now been imparted to the church, which Paul called the mystical body of Christ. The church is the sole repository of the supernatural wisdom of Christ in the earth because it is the only company of people who have received the "spirit of wisdom and revelation." God's intention is that "through the church, the manifold wisdom of God should be made known" (Ephesians 3:10).

The ancient story of the Queen of Sheba travelling from afar to listen to the wisdom of Solomon is a powerful prophetic picture of something that God clearly desires and intends for the church in our day. As the manifold wisdom of God is poured out upon those who are actively seeking Him for greater wisdom in the pastoral and healing ministry, God has purposed in His heart to release such a depth of prophetic insight into the human condition and an anointing of power to set the captives free. Even the leaders of the therapeutic community will come to the church to listen to the prophetic knowledge of the heart that God is unveiling in the saints. Has not God called the church to **teach the nations** everything that He has prophetically revealed through His Son, Jesus Christ? The church has a glorious prophetic mandate to teach the nations, and this includes the therapeutic community.

If the church walked in just a fraction of the wisdom and power of Jesus, we would astonish the secular therapeutic community. God's intention is to make known His manifold wisdom through the church. Did you catch that? Read that again without the cloak of religious familiarity, which so often veils our reading of the Scriptures: **God**, the Creator of the heavens and the earth, intends to make known **His** supreme, supernatural wisdom through a company of people on earth who are actively contending for an unparalleled outpouring of the Spirit of wisdom and revelation.

"If any of you lacks wisdom, he should ask God, who gives generously to all ... and it will be given to him" (James 1:5). James is speaking about "the wisdom that comes from heaven" (James 3:17 NIV). This is a supernatural wisdom that streams forth from the very heart and mind of an all-knowing God who has a thorough and comprehensive knowledge of the condition of my heart. This extraordinary prophetic wisdom powerfully eclipses the best so-called "wisdom" of the world. The wisdom that comes from above reflects the heaven to earth model of ministry that the Lord is restoring to the church in this day. We will close this book with a final chapter on the profound implications of the emerging heaven to earth model of ministry.

Paul had a comprehensive vision for the supernatural wisdom of Christ to expose the foolishness of earthly wisdom. He lived in a day when the Greek philosophers had so exalted their earthly, human wisdom that some of the Corinthian believers were finding themselves intimidated by their sophistry and their oratorical prowess. Paul had to address this issue in the church because the Corinthians were beginning to exalt the earthly wisdom of Greek philosophy above the wisdom of Christ that was demonstrated in the cross. Paul wrote stinging words to expose the arrogance of this earthly wisdom. "For it is written: 'I will destroy the wisdom of the wise, and bring to nothing the understanding of the prudent'" (1 Corinthians 1:19). The next verse in the New Living Translation continues, "So where does this leave the philosophers, the scholars, and the world's brilliant debaters? God has made them all look foolish and has shown their wisdom to be useless nonsense" (1 Corinthians 1:20 NLT). "For the wisdom of this world is foolishness with God" (1 Corinthians 3:19).

We are told in the Book of Kings that when the Queen of Sheba beheld the extraordinary wisdom of Solomon, "there was no more spirit in her" (1 Kings 10:5). This encounter with divine wisdom left her "breathless" and "overwhelmed" as other translations put it. I can relate to this. My own encounter with the prophetic wisdom of Christ has left me breathless and stunned on many occasions. If we are thoroughly enamoured with the earthly wisdom of secular therapists who seek to heal the soul with mere talk therapy, it begs the question if we have yet caught a glimpse of the glorious kingdom ministry of Christ.

Paul was clearly overwhelmed by the revelation of Christ, the wisdom of God. He counselled everyone under his apostolic care to actively pray for an outpouring of the "spirit of wisdom and revelation in the knowledge of Christ." Paul said, "I pray also that the eyes of your heart may be enlightened in order that you may *know*" (Ephesians 1:17-18). There is a supernatural *knowing* that God deposits in the hearts of the humble and contrite. John said, "We *know* that the Son of God has come and has given us an *understanding*, that we *may know* Him who is true" (1 John 5:20). The Greek word for *understanding* is *dianoia*, which means deep thought.[41] This deep, prophetic understanding parallels Paul's concept of "depth of insight" (Philippians 1:9 NIV), which is a supernatural perception that results from revelatory encounter. As a result of our eyes being opened by God, we come to a place in the Spirit where we actually *know* through a prophetic encounter with the living God.

Psychotherapy is the art of healing the soul. The term is made up of two Greek words: *psyche* and *therapeuo*. It means *the cure of souls*, and this has historically been the domain of the church. A "curate" is an archaic English term for a clergyman. The primary means of administering this supernatural art of healing has been the application of the wisdom, love, and power of God to the brokenness of humanity. Secular psychotherapy has claimed the high moral ground and has robbed this ministry from the church. Too many saints are intimidated by this Goliath. The power of this intimidation lies in its use of technical language and its self-assumed authority. But why should the saints of the Most High be intimidated by mere human wisdom when our heritage is the wisdom and the power of the Holy Spirit? Why should secular therapists be revered as the new high priests of mental and emotional healing? Why should they be the head and not the tail?

It is God's glorious intention that His church becomes the head and not the tail in the ministry of healing the soul. "If you listen to these commands of the Lord your God and carefully obey them, the Lord will make you the head and not the tail, and you will always have the upper hand" (Deuteronomy 28:13 NLT). Another translation says, "You will always be at the top; never at the bottom" (NIV). This is not a fair competition! According to the Scriptures, the saints have unlimited access to the resources of heaven, whereas secular therapists only have access to mere human wisdom with absolutely no revelation of the power of the cross, the reality of the new creation, the power to overcome the demonic realm, the healing power of the unconditional love of the Father, or the operation of the Spirit of prophecy. These are the tools and gifts at our disposal if we would only learn how to administer them. Paul spoke directly to this issue when he said,

> My message and my preaching were not with wise and persuasive words of human wisdom, but with a demonstration of the Spirit's power, so that your faith might not rest on men's wisdom, but on God's power. We do, however, speak a message of wisdom among the mature, but not the wisdom of this age or of the rulers of this age, who are coming to

nothing. No, we speak of God's secret wisdom, a wisdom that has been hidden and that God destined for our glory before time began (1 Corinthians 2:4-7 NIV).

Paul intentionally juxtaposed the supernatural ministry of the Holy Spirit with a ministry that is built upon mere earthly wisdom. His point is that there is no comparison. Christ has come and everything must now revolve itself around this single revelation. Any promise of healing that is not anchored in this revelation ends up becoming smoke and mirrors. It may claim to offer authentic healing, but if it only offers the psychological re-programming of what Paul called the "old man," then it is merely seeking to put a patch on an old garment. Paul said, "Neither circumcision nor uncircumcision means anything; what counts is a new creation" (Galatians 6:15). The supernatural new creation miracle is the starting point for our personal transformation. It is the foundation of all spiritual healing.

Secular psychology has done the church a great service in identifying and explaining the broad spectrum of human psychological and behavioral disorders. Through the systematic observation of patterns of human brokenness, the science of human psychology has arrived at a body of empirical knowledge that is beyond dispute. They have applied a scientific methodology to observe these obvious patterns of human mental, emotional, and psychological dysfunctions. Their conclusion is essentially the same as the earnest student of the Scriptures. To one degree or another, human beings are all desperately broken and our lives are troubled by various psychological, spiritual, and emotional disorders. No one can argue with this observation. But when secular psychologists endeavour to apply their wisdom and knowledge to the healing of the soul, things inevitably go astray.

While we honour the aspirations of the psycho-therapeutic community to heal the soul, those of us who are trained by the Spirit to place no confidence in the flesh, question the capacity of secular psychotherapists to deliver on their promise. To seek to resolve deep problems of living, apart from the pursuit of God, is a quest that is doomed to fail. The true healing of the soul is the by-product of seeking to know God and, as we have already seen, the revelatory knowledge of God is the foundation of the transformation and the renovation of the heart. The first step on this journey is to be converted to Christ and to become a new creation in Him. Then God begins to unveil the heart of Christ in us. This is the only true foundation of genuine spiritual change. "For no one can lay any foundation other than the one already laid, which is Jesus Christ" (1 Corinthians 3:11 NIV).

Christ alone is the only true Psychotherapist. He is the only true Healer of our soul. He has His own school of heavenly psychotherapy, which does not need to be supplemented by human wisdom or technique. And His ministry is not to produce a *changed* life but an *exchanged* life. As Paul said, "I have been crucified with Christ; it is no longer I who lives, but Christ who lives in me" (Galatians 2:20). The only solution for the "old man" is the power of the cross. Only here is the flesh supernaturally crucified and the old nature circumcised or cut away from the human heart. Paul called it "the cutting away of your sinful nature" (Colossians 2:11 NLT). Psychotherapists know absolutely nothing of this miracle new birth. Tragically, very few believers know anything about it either.

Let's take this discussion one step further by asking if the secular psycho-therapeutic community is in any way advancing the agenda of heaven. Mature Christians understand that God uses people's descent into deeper brokenness to bring them to the end of themselves so they will cry out for the mercy of God and become receptive to the overtures of divine grace. What happens when a psychotherapist interrupts this process by dazzling their client with their professional psychobabble? They send him or her away with new management tools and a greater sense of self esteem in the midst of their personal apocalypse.

Has that therapist helped to bring that person one step closer to God or have they interrupted the process by making the client feel better about themselves, merely making them *feel* happier? How does heaven perceive the most well intentioned secular psychotherapist or counsellor? The more we think about this, the more apparent it becomes that the agenda of secular psychotherapy actually works against the agenda of heaven. God seeks to use people's ever deepening descent into sin and emotional brokenness as a tool to break them. God seeks to humble them with the realization of their weakness and to bring them to their knees.

The gospel message of Paul resulted in genuine freedom at the core of people's hearts. He built communities of people who came together under the power of his revolutionary gospel preaching. He started new creation communities that were colonies of heaven. He raised up an army of transformed men and women who enjoyed the fruits of the Spirit and who ministered in the power of the Spirit. These communities were a city set upon a hill, and they only existed because the people in these communities purposed to respond to Paul's call to become a people who "lived from the heart."

Paul said, "Do we need, like some people, letters of recommendation to you or from you? *You yourselves are our letter*, written on our hearts, known and read by everybody. You show that you are a letter from Christ, *the result of our ministry*, written not with ink but with the Spirit of the living God, not on tablets of stone but on tablets of human hearts" (2 Corinthians 3:1-3 NIV). Paul's letters of commendation were people whose hearts and lives were transformed through the power of his gospel.

No one can argue with genuine fruit. Jesus said, "Wisdom is justified by her children" (Matthew 11:19). In another translation, "Wisdom is shown to be right by what results from it" (NIV). The Holy Spirit is actively seeking to unveil the glory Christ's kingdom ministry by inwardly transforming His people through the wisdom, power, and love of God. As the saints walk in supernatural wisdom, their lives take on a radiance and a splendor that speaks prophetically to those who dwell in darkness. This is the prophetic promise of Isaiah 60.

> Arise, shine; for your light has come! And the glory of the Lord is risen upon you. For behold, the darkness shall cover the earth, and deep darkness the people; but the Lord will arise over you, and His glory will be seen upon you.[42] All nations will come to your light. Mighty kings will come to see your radiance. Look and see, for everyone is coming home! Your sons are coming from distant lands; your little daughters will be carried home.[43] Then you will see and be radiant, and your heart will thrill and rejoice; because the abundance of the sea will be turned to you, the wealth of the nations will come to you" (Isaiah 60:1-5).

This passage is reminiscent of the story of the Queen of Sheba bringing her wealth to the feet of King Solomon. God always seeks to display His glory in His transformed people. As we have just said, no one can argue with genuine fruit. This principle flows throughout the Scriptures. "I will show how holy My great name is ... and when I reveal **My holiness through you** before their very eyes, says the Sovereign Lord, then the nations will know that I am the Lord" (Ezekiel 36:23). God not only seeks to unveil His holiness in His people, He also seeks to unveil His wholeness. This wholeness is manifested in His love being poured out in the lives of His people. Love only flows out of those who are in the process of being made whole. "By this all will know that you are My disciples, if you have love for one another" (John 13:35).

The authentic love of Christ worked into the hearts of His followers is a rare commodity on the earth and it speaks prophetically to the nations. The outpouring of love and harmony amongst the people of God is the crowning achievement of God's great redemption. It is this love that creates the "city set upon a hill" that cannot be hidden. This is what Jesus prayed for in His High Priestly prayer. His intent was that this uncommon love would speak prophetically to the nations so that they would believe.

> I do not pray for these alone, but also for those who will believe in Me through their word; that they all may be one, as You, Father, are in Me, and I in You; that they also may be one in Us, ***that the world may believe*** that You sent Me. And the glory which You gave Me I have given them, that they may be one just as We are one: I in them, and You in Me; that they may be made perfect in one, and ***that the world may know*** that You have sent Me, and have loved them as You have loved Me (John 17:20-23).

As the saints embrace the call to discipleship, to take up their cross to follow Christ, God is faithful to transform His people into the very image of Christ. This fruit speaks powerfully to the nations. There is tremendous power in the revelation of spiritual community. The perfect love of Christ casts out all fear. His love delivers us from all shame. There is no greater revelation of the glory of the Lord than the people of God emerging into holiness, personal wholeness, and genuine community. "Come, let us tell of the Lord's greatness; let us exalt His name together. I prayed to the Lord, and He answered me, freeing me from all my fears. Those who look to Him for help will be radiant with joy; no shadow of shame will darken their faces" (Psalm 34:3-5 NIV). In the end, it is not our beliefs that make the church the head and not the tail. It is the fruit of the Holy Spirit in our lives and no one can argue with genuine fruit. "Wisdom is shown to be right by what results from it" (Matthew 11:19 NIV).

Chapter Twelve

The Implications of the "Heaven to Earth" Paradigm

> This then, is how you should pray: "Your kingdom come,
> Your will be done on earth as it is in heaven."
> (Matthew 6:10)

In chapter ten we introduced the idea of an apostolic reformation that is beginning to take place in the church. In this historically significant reformation, God is restoring to the church an apostolic paradigm of ministry that is built upon the concept of ***heaven invading earth***. Part of this apostolic reformation includes the full restoration of a heaven to earth model of kingdom ministry. Jesus clearly taught that His church should be contending through prayer for heaven to invade earth in every sphere of human existence. He taught us to pray, "Your kingdom come; Your will be done on earth as it is in heaven" (Matthew 6:10). This is especially true for every aspect of ministry to the heart.

It is evident that not all Christians embrace the radicalism of the heaven to earth model of ministry. For various reasons, whether it is a lack of biblical revelation, blindness induced by relentless satanic attack, or the descent into a gloomy and pessimistic acceptance of personal defeat in relation to issues of the heart, many Christians are not living out of the perspective that Jesus outlined when He taught His disciples to pray. The notion that "with God all things are possible" challenges every negative and pessimistic mind-set with the truth that Jesus has come to set right all things that are wrong from the perspective of heaven.

If we are serious about embracing the heaven to earth model of ministry, we must allow it to impact every sphere of Christian ministry. The heaven to earth model has profound implications for every sphere of ministry that touches upon the human heart. Churches that embrace an apostolic ministry model of heaven invading earth have a responsibility to ensure that the model of personal transformation that they adopt and promote is exclusively from above and free from any intermingling with what James called "earthly wisdom" (see James 3:15). Whenever there is an infiltration of earthly wisdom into the church's model of ministry, it inevitably becomes in some way distorted and perverted from the original heavenly blueprint.

There are some extremely revolutionary threads of revelation emerging in the midst of this current apostolic reformation. Bill Johnson, one of the most influential leaders of this present reformation, is well known for a simple but profound saying, "Jesus Christ is perfect theology." Of course, Jesus is the standard of all true biblical theology because He is the Word of God who became flesh and blood. If a particular theology or model of ministry doesn't perfectly resemble Jesus, then it is a sub-standard reality – a reality that fails to reflect the full radicalism of Jesus in what He has come to establish upon the earth. Everything we believe and practice as followers of Christ needs to be subjected to the rigorous scrutiny of Jesus' perfect heavenly ministry. We study the Word of God but we need to be equally aware that the Word of God studies us. It evaluates whether we are building with wood, hay, and stubble or with gold, silver, and precious stones.

The Implications of the "Heaven to Earth" Paradigm

Jesus said, "As the Father has sent Me, so I send you" (John 20:21 NLT). The *Amplified Bible* reads, "Just as the Father has sent Me forth, so I am sending you." The Greek word for sent is *apostello*, and it means to be sent on a mission with a specific mandate. The Father sent Jesus on a specific mission with a specific ministry mandate. That mandate was to invade the earth with the full reality of heaven and to bring the kingdom of heaven down to earth in its fullness. That is why Jesus is called ***the*** Apostle (Hebrews 3:1). He is the archetype of all true apostolic ministry. His ministry scrutinizes our ministry. In exactly the same manner that Jesus was sent forth by the Father with an apostolic mandate, so now, Jesus sends us forth with exactly the same heavenly mandate. The invention of self styled models of Christian ministry, nowhere more powerfully expressed than in the integrationist movement, reveals the fact that many followers of Jesus have failed to come to grips with the full radicalism of the apostolic paradigm. There is a heavenly blueprint of pure kingdom ministry that comes exclusively from above, and the powers of darkness have fought for centuries to obscure or diminish the radicalism of this apostolic model of kingdom ministry. Only now, in the early part of the twenty-first century, are we beginning to see the dawn of a new era of ministry that restores the heaven to earth paradigm.

All thoughtful followers of Jesus who are concerned with issues of biblical fidelity should pause to meditate upon the profound implications of this paradigm shift. We need to allow the heaven to earth model to scrutinize the presuppositions and the praxis of contemporary ministry. The reformation is not yet complete! New light is continually breaking in upon the church as the various threads of revelation are interwoven into a comprehensive vision of heaven invading earth. The big apostolic paradigm is made up of multiple threads of revelation that create a tapestry. The missing pieces of the big picture leave us with a deficient vision of what it means for God's kingdom to come on earth, just as it is in heaven. God wants the fullness of

His will to be done in your heart and mine, just as it is in heaven. My greatest concern in writing this book, which seeks to recover the biblical knowledge of the heart, is to bring into focus the necessity of allowing the radicalism of Jesus' ministry to the human heart to challenge the status quo and to scrutinize everything that passes for Christian ministry. God wants Jesus' ministry to be restored to centre stage. We have emphasized that Jesus has a perfect ministry that does not need to be supplemented by earthly wisdom or secular theories of human personality. I have endeavoured to make the distinction between these two philosophies of ministry as clear as I can. I have repeatedly sought to contrast the heavenly model of ministry against the backdrop of a prevailing religious culture, which has adopted "pearls" of earthly wisdom to supplement a perceived lack in the church's ministry of personal transformation.

Jesus walks in the midst of the church and He navigates an environment where His own supernatural ministry of deep heart transformation has often been eclipsed by earthly models of ministry. My primary passion in writing this present series of books is to recover the fullness of this biblical sphere of knowledge and to point the church toward the full recovery of Jesus' ministry of bringing about a supernatural transformation of the human heart. What we really believe will ultimately shape our ministry praxis, so if we are not seeing the full picture we are in urgent need of an upgrade in our vision.

The second volume in this series focuses upon what I have chosen to call the "new creation miracle." The first thing Jesus does in His great plan of personal redemption is to make every person who puts their trust in Him into an entirely new creation. This new birth is an extraordinary miracle, and it sets the stage for all subsequent transformation. The miracle of the regeneration of the human heart through the resurrection power of Jesus Christ represents the foundation and cornerstone of all spiritual change in the heart of the believer.

The Implications of the "Heaven to Earth" Paradigm

Secular psychotherapists, with their unbiblical theories of human personality, (along with their Christian integrationist cousins who take their cues from the secular theorists), fail to come to terms with the full implications of the miracle of a brand new spirit and a brand new heart. Without this powerful revelation, they are endlessly putting a new patch on an old garment. Instead of calling out the new identity that God has given His adopted sons and daughters, secular therapists are forever seeking to modify the engine, rather than completely replacing it. The Lord said through Ezekiel the prophet, "Get yourselves a new heart and a new spirit" (Ezekiel 18:31).

In the end it is all a matter of perspective. The most critical issue is: how does God see us in Christ? From heaven's perspective every born again believer in Jesus is an entirely new creation. A supernatural creative act has occurred in their human spirit and the old has quite literally passed away. This new creation miracle is the only foundation that Christ can proceed to build upon. The new birth is the first decisive strike of heaven invading earth.

The goal of all ministry to the heart, whether secular or Christian, is to affect change on the inside of a person, so that the person suffering from significant problems of living can begin to move forward in their personal lives and enter into freedom. Within the church, most integrationist models of ministry tend to seriously underestimate the sweeping ramifications of the miracle of the new birth, focusing more attention upon equipping people with greater life skills or tools for better management of their personal issues.

Paul, the champion of New Testament new creation theology, emphasized that all new creations in Christ are now heavenly beings. Paul contrasted new creations with *the natural man* (1 Corinthians 2:14), suggesting a super-natural dimension to the life of the believer. Born again believers are an entirely new order of human being and are no longer defined by *natural* attributes. In Romans, Paul said there were now two kinds of humans: those who are in Adam and those who are in Christ. These two men are the spiritual heads of two races of humans. "For if, by the trespass of the one man, death reigned through that one man, how much more will those who receive God's abundant provision of grace and of the gift of righteousness reign in life through the one man, Jesus Christ" (Romans 5:17 NIV). In 1 Corinthians, Paul develops this idea further by using the language of "heavenly" versus "earthly."

> So it is written, "The first man Adam became a living being." The last Adam became a life-giving Spirit. However, the spiritual is not first, but the natural, and afterward the spiritual. The first man was of the earth, made of dust; the second Man is the Lord from heaven. As was the man of dust, so also are those who are made of dust; and as is the heavenly Man, so also are those who are heavenly. And as we have borne the image of the man of dust, we shall also bear the image of the heavenly Man (1 Corinthians 15:46-49).

Paul said that those who are "in Christ" are now heavenly men and women. He described all New Testament believers as "those who **are heavenly!**" Jesus is the "firstborn among many brethren" (Romans 8:29). If Jesus is described as the "heavenly Man," then we are also fully-fledged "heavenly" men and women. Jesus spoke of Himself as dwelling in heaven even while He was upon the earth. "No one has ascended to heaven but He who came down from heaven, that is, the Son of Man **who is in heaven**" (John 3:13).

If Jesus is the firstborn amongst many brethren, then we can safely say that if anyone is in Christ, he or she is also simultaneously "in heaven" even though they are physically located on earth. We are bi-locational beings because we are now in two places at the same time. Paul said, "For our citizenship is in heaven" (Philippians 3:20). According to Paul, "God raised us up with Christ and seated us with Him in the heavenly realms in Christ Jesus" (Ephesians 2:6 NIV).

The Implications of the "Heaven to Earth" Paradigm

All of this has significant implications for the nature of ministry to those who have become new creations in Christ. Paul said explicitly, "We judge thus: that if One died for all, then all died; and He died for all, that those who live should live no longer for themselves, but for Him who died for them and rose again. Therefore, from now on, we regard no one according to the flesh" (2 Corinthians 5:14-16). We are not to know our fellow Christians according to their old selfish, sinful nature. We are to know them as brand new creations and to prophetically speak to the treasure inside each and every believer.

It is amazing how, through lack of biblical revelation, we continue to relate to one another in Christ as though nothing significant has changed on the inside. We are under obligation to reckon others and ourselves in Christ as being dead to sin and gloriously alive to God (Romans 6:11). Any model or philosophy of ministry that is not founded firmly on the revelation of the new creation is an unbiblical model. God is not interested in the ***changed life***: He is all about the ***exchanged life*** where we die so that Christ lives in us in all His radiant glory. Paul said, "I have been crucified with Christ; it is no longer I who live, but Christ lives in me" (Galatians 2:20).

All who are called to minister are also called to treat their brothers and sisters in Christ as heavenly beings. How do we minister to heavenly men and heavenly women? Well, that all depends on how much someone has had their mind renewed by heaven's perspective. The apostolic paradigm of ministry places infinitely greater emphasis upon unveiling whom we are in Christ, rather than in speaking to the garbage and the brokenness in the lives of those who are being supernaturally transformed into the image of Christ. This doesn't mean that we completely ignore issues of sin or brokenness in the church. Jesus certainly didn't in His letters to the seven churches in the book of Revelation. These issues are real!

In the book of Hebrews, the Father disciplines His sons and daughters. He does this through loving correction, discipline, reproof, and sometimes rebuke. "The Lord disciplines those He loves, and He punishes everyone He accepts as a son" (Hebrews 12:6 NIV). This is reminiscent of the words of Jesus when He said, "Those whom I love I rebuke and discipline" (Revelation 3:19). We do not ignore strongholds of sin and emotional brokenness in the life of the believer but we address these issues through the lens of the new creation, pointing out that certain behaviors and responses are significantly beneath the dignity of new creations in Christ. God does indeed correct sons and daughters of heaven when they continue to behave like sons and daughters of earth.

The first thing Jesus does in ministering to those who come to Him for salvation is to re-create them on the inside and give them a brand new nature and a brand new core identity. This is the first step in kingdom ministry. As John Peterson (1921-2006) wrote in this beloved hymn:

> Heaven came down and glory filled my soul, when at the ~~first~~ [cross] my Saviour made me whole. My sins were washed away and my night turned into day, when heaven came down and glory filled my soul!

While we spend the rest of our lives becoming who we already are in Christ, all spiritual transformation in our heart flows out of the glorious new birth. This is axiomatic to all authentic New Testament ministry.

So I invite you to journey with me into the second book in this series where we will begin to explore the biblical model of supernatural transformation through the lens of the glorious kingdom ministry of Jesus. This heavenly model of transformation begins with the new creation miracle. In the next book, we will explore this powerful New Testament theme by seeking to plumb the depths of Paul's theology of the new creation in all its glory. My experience of over thirty years as a Christian is that the true gospel of the new creation is frequently misunderstood, distorted, and obscured by religion.

The Implications of the "Heaven to Earth" Paradigm

In the next book, we will seek to come to terms with the sheer majesty of this supernatural invasion of heaven to earth in the hearts of the sons and daughters of God. The glorious new creation miracle is the foundation of all change in the life of the Christian. We are living in a period of church history where this powerful apostolic message is being recovered once again. I promise you: book two will be a mind-blowing experience as we see just how heaven has invaded earth in the human heart.

Every Christian needs a strong dose of this heavenly medicine so that we can think straight about the critical issue of the supernatural transformation of our hearts. The more clearly we can see what it is that God has done and what He wants to do, the more we can cooperate with Him in His unrelenting agenda to conform us to the image of Jesus in this life. That the glory of Christ may cover the earth as the waters cover the sea – one heart at a time!

Endnotes

1. T. Sorg, "Heart", *Dictionary of New Testament Theology,* Vol. 2, p. 182
2. G.E. Ladd, *A Theology of the New Testament,* p. 475
3. Colin Brown, *Dictionary of New Testament Theology,* Vol. 2, pp. 181-182
4. Mark Heard, "I Just Wanna Get Warm" from the *Second Hand* album (1991)
5. Mike Bickle, *Passion For Jesus* pp. 49-50
6. A.W. Tozer, *The Knowledge of the Holy* pp. 6, 7, 10
7. ibid, pp. 11-12
8. Bickle, op. cit. pp. 54, 56-57
9. ibid, pp. 100, 101, 103
10. Gordon & Gail MacDonald, *Heart Connections,* p. 18
11. ibid, pp. 33-34, 35-36
12. Larry Crabb, *Understanding People,* pp. 194-197
13. I attribute this teaching on the relationship between intimacy and analysis to John Arnott of the Toronto Airport Christian Fellowship, Toronto, Canada.
14. A.W. Tozer, *Faith Beyond Reason,* p. 24
15. Charles Finney, *The Backslider in Heart*
16. Bob Sorge, *Secrets of the Secret Place,* pp. 200-201
17. ibid, pp. 19-20
18. Ed Bulkley, *Why Christians Can't Trust Psychology,* p. 166
19. A. V. Campbell [Editor], *Dictionary Of Pastoral Care,* p. 12
20. ibid
21. Larry Crabb, *Understanding People,* p. 142
22. ibid, p. 12
23. Sigmund Freud, *On Metapsychology: The Theory of Psychoanalysis,* pp. 390-391
24. David Powlison, "Integration or Inundation?" in *Power Religion: The Selling Out of the Evangelical Church,* p. 192
25. ibid, p. 193
26. ibid, p. 197
27. ibid, p. 198
28. Os Guinness, "America's Last Men and Their Magnificent Talking Cure", *No God but God: Breaking With the Idols of Our Age,* p. 115

29. ibid, p. 117
30. ibid, p. 114
31. Jim Owen, *Christian Psychology's War on God's Word,* p. 207
32. Gary S. Greig & Kevin N. Springer, "Introduction", *The Kingdom and the Power,* p. 21
33. ibid, p. 34
34. David Powlison, "Integration or Inundation?" in *Power Religion: The Selling Out of the Evangelical Church,* p. 213
35. ibid, p. 207.
36. "Homoousios" means **of the same substance** and was used to describe the nature of Christ and the Father. The Emperor Constantine proposed this word at the Council of Nicea in 325 AD. This word found its way into the Nicene creed, which was accepted by the West but ultimately rejected by the East, resulting in the schism in the church.
37. Luke 2:46-47
38. Matthew 7:28, 22:23; Mark 1:22, 11:18; Luke 4:32
39. Matthew 4:24-25
40. See the definition of "dianoia" in the Strong's Concordance, G1271
41. NKJV
42. NIV
43. NNAS

Bibliography

Mike Bickle, *Passion For Jesus* (Charisma House, 1996).

Colin Brown, editor, *New International Dictionary of New Testament Theology* (Zondervan, 1986).

Ed Bulkley, *Why Christians Can't Trust Psychology* (Harvest House, 1993).

Charles Colson, editor, *Power Religion: The Selling out of the Evangelical Church* (Moody Press, 1997).

A. V. Campbell, editor, *Dictionary Of Pastoral Care* (Crossroad Publishing Company 1987).

Larry Crabb, *Understanding People* (Zondervan, 1987).

Charles Finney, *The Backslider in Heart* (Available on the Internet, Public Domain).

Sigmund Freud, *On Metapsychology: The Theory of Psychoanalysis* (Penguin Books, 1991).

G.S. Greig & Kevin N. Springer, *The Kingdom and the Power* (Regal Books, 1993).

Os Guinness & John Seel, editors, *No God but God: Breaking With The Idols of Our Age* (Moody Press, 1992).

G. E. Ladd, *A Theology of the New Testament* (Eerdmans Publishing Company, 1993).

Gordon & Gail MacDonald, *Heart Connections: Growing Intimacy in Your Marriage and Family* (Fleming H. Revell Company 1997).

Jim Owen, *Christian Psychology's War on God's Word* (Timeless Texts, 2004).

Bob Sorge, *Secrets of the Secret Place* (Oasis House, 2001).

A. W. Tozer, *Faith Beyond Reason* (Wingspread Publishing, 2009).

A. W. Tozer, *The Knowledge of the Holy* (Harper One, 1978).

NEW EARTH TRIBE

Phil and Maria Mason are the Spiritual Directors of ***New Earth Tribe***, a spiritual community that began in 1998 and is located in Byron Bay, Australia. Since 2006, this community has experienced a sustained outpouring of supernatural ministry. Byron Bay is world renowned as a centre of New Age spirituality. As Phil and Maria tell it, "Finding ourselves in the midst of the New Age marketplace, we have developed a passion to penetrate the culture with the supernatural healing power of Christ. As we have pressed into this goal, we have experienced a significant outpouring of healing, which has released an ecstatic atmosphere over our community. The more we live in the atmosphere of the supernatural, the more we are elevated into a state of spiritual ecstasy – and we were made for ecstasy!

Whenever Jesus healed the sick, those who witnessed the miracles were astonished and amazed. Jesus called these miracles signs and wonders. They were tangible signs of the invasion of the kingdom of heaven that induced a sense of astonishment, joy, and wonder. Revival culture is sustained by a continued outpouring of these signs and wonders, much like the community of believers in the book of Acts. The outpouring of the Spirit is always accompanied by an outpouring of authentic joy and ecstasy.

The greatest core values of the Tribe are community and intimacy. We have been on a fourteen-year journey into spiritual community, and we are finding more and more that true fulfilment in God is only enjoyed in the context of committed relationships. Any good fruit that has come out of our community is a result of an unswerving commitment to real, accountable friendships that are both loving and truthful. We truly love the power of community and we wholeheartedly preach it as the foundation for lasting revival.

Our journey has also seen an explosion of wild worship and unique creativity that has accompanied the outpouring of the supernatural. We are committed to the journey of becoming an authentic "Book of Acts" community in the 21st century that turns the world upside down!

To find out more about this community, please visit our website:
www.newearthtribe.com

DEEP END SCHOOL OF THE SUPERNATURAL

Phil and Maria are the directors and founders of the ***Deep End School of the Supernatural***. This nine month, part-time school, founded in 2003, trains people of all ages in the Kingdom Ministry of Jesus Christ. One of the unique features of this ministry is the importance placed upon contextualisation. Students are trained to understand New Age and Postmodern culture and to develop an intelligent response to the explosion of this culture. Students develop a model of ministry that takes into account the unique challenges created by the emergence of radical postmodernism with its categorical rejection of absolute truth. Oftentimes Christian ministry in the twenty-first century lacks this contextualisation of the gospel.

The Deep End School is empowered by a specific ministry philosophy. The shift from the modernist era to the post-modernist era represents a transition away from words that describe reality to the subjective experience of reality. We are now living in a "show me" generation, rather than a "tell me" generation. As a result, people are fatigued by a "word only" approach to marketing spirituality. They want to see tangible demonstrations of the world we are attempting to describe.

We have found that the kingdom ministry of Christ is the key to penetrating the hearts of post-modern seekers. Post-modernists have been awakened to the reality of supernatural power and spiritual experience. Subsequently, the Deep End School trains students to heal the sick, break demonic bondages, heal broken hearts, and flow in the prophetic. As an extension of this approach to ministry, the school trains its students to release the glory realm of heaven through true, supernatural encounters with God that usher people into the ecstasy realm.

Post-modern seekers are hungry for authentic spiritual encounters that open up the realm of ecstasy and bliss. That is why they are flocking to New Age practitioners who offer their adherents an experience of supernatural power. New Age and post-modern seekers intentionally bypass expressions of spirituality that cannot deliver an encounter. It is time to give this generation an encounter with the living God. He will rise up a generation of ecstatic lovers of Christ.

To find out more about this nine month school, please visit our website:

www.deependschool.com

Other Books by Phil Mason

Quantum Glory: The Science of Heaven Invading Earth

Quantum Glory explores the intriguing intersection between the two realities of quantum mechanics and the glory of God. Part one of the book explores how the sub-atomic world is a revelation of exceptionally intricate divine design that unveils the mind of our Creator. In part two, the author explains exactly how the glory of God invades our physical universe to affect miracles of divine healing. This book is packed with revelation that is guaranteed to blow your mind. But more than that, it is designed to equip you in supernatural ministry so that you can also release the glory of God on earth as it is in heaven!

The real glory of this book is that it gives understanding of this wonderful world around us in a way that creates awe for what God has done. It also ignites praise in our hearts to the Creator of all, while at the same time giving us understanding of how things work. God left His message everywhere for anyone interested in truth. His fingerprints are everywhere: from the largest galaxies in existence, to the smallest thing known to man. I appreciate Phil's amazing insights and deep understanding of very difficult subjects addressed in **Quantum Glory**. I am especially thankful for his gift of taking big thoughts and breaking them down so that all of us can understand them. But I am also glad for how He values mystery. Anything that creates awe and wonder, all the while pointing to Jesus, to me is priceless. With that note, I highly recommend **Quantum Glory**. Enjoy. Be awed. Give God praise over and over again.

Bill Johnson
Senior Pastor, Bethel Church, Redding, California USA

God is still creating ways for His people to respond to His overtures. All creation speaks of Him and the language and principles of quantum physics are a vital part of His heavenly discourse with humanity. From quantum non-locality through sound waves, string theory, the mathematical order of nature, quantum geometry and the golden ratio, to the alignment between quantum physics and the supernatural, the glory of God and the key to miracles; you will understand more about the radiant nature of God in this book than in any other tome that is specifically non-specific. I heartily recommend Phil Mason to you as a leader in the field of modern day spirituality, the new sciences and the supernatural gospel of the Lord Jesus Christ.

Graham Cooke,
Author, Prophetic Speaker and Owner of Brilliant Book House.com

We are in the midst of a worldwide move of God with signs and wonders breaking out all over the world. In **Quantum Glory,** Phil Mason combines his passion for the science of quantum physics with his personal wealth of experience in supernatural ministry and sound Biblical theology. The result is an explosive mix of revelation that has the potential to powerfully envision and activate you to alter the very fabric of the physical world around you through the healing ministry of Christ. This book fills a vital gap in the literature that is emerging in this present wave of revival.

Dr. Che Ahn
President, Harvest International Ministry
International Chancellor, Wagner Leadership Institute

The Supernatural Transformation Series

If you have enjoyed reading this book, Phil Mason has also written three additional volumes on the theme of the Supernatural Transformation of the Heart. This series outlines a supernatural Kingdom Ministry based model of personal transformation. God seeks to transform our hearts from the inside out as we embrace the call to a deep heart journey of intimacy with God and one another in spiritual community.

This profound theology of the heart puts in place all the conceptual building blocks for deep, personal transformation. It begins with the miracle of the new creation and it unfolds the process of transformation from one degree of glory to another as we allow God to demolish every stronghold of the mind, will, and emotions so that we can be gloriously transformed into the very image of Christ. The context of this transformation is spiritual community that values genuine supernatural encounter with Christ.

Volume 1:

The Knowledge of the Heart

Volume 2:

The New Creation Miracle

Volume 3:

The Heart Journey

Volume 4:

The Glory of God and Supernatural Transformation

AUTHOR'S CONTACT INFORMATION:

www.philmason.org

Phil's website also contains a large selection of his unique teaching materials with downloadable mp3s, individual CDs, CD sets, and DVDs, which can be ordered through his store. PayPal, Master Card, and Visa Card facilities are available for safe online transactions. We ship worldwide. Additional postage and shipping charges apply.

Australia and New Zealand: Please order books through Phil's website. To obtain bulk quantities for bookstores, please contact Phil Mason by writing to:

> Phil Mason,
> PO Box 1627,
> Byron Bay, New South Wales, Australia, 2481

or contact the author by email at: sales@philmason.org

ORDERING INFORMATION

Additional copies of this book and other resources by Phil Mason as well as other XP Publishing books, are available at the "store" at XPministries.com, Amazon, and your local Christian store, upon request.

Wholesale prices for stores and ministries

Please contact:
usaresource@xpministries.com.

In Canada, please contact:
resource@xpministries.com.

Australia and New Zealand:
www.philmason.org
(Please see complete information on page 232).

XP Publishing books are also available to wholesale and retail stores through anchordistributors.com

www.XPPublishing.com
XP Ministries